YOUR LAST SELF-HELP BOOK

A Common-Sense Approach to Living Life on Your Terms

GLYNIS TAYLOR

First published by Ultimate World Publishing 2020
Copyright © 2020 Glynis Taylor

ISBN

Paperback - 978-1-922372-00-0
Ebook - 978-1-922372-01-7

Glynis Taylor has asserted her rights under the Copyright, Designs and Patents Act 1988 to be identified as the author of this work. The information in this book is based on the author's experiences and opinions. The publisher specifically disclaims responsibility for any adverse consequences, which may result from use of the information contained herein. Permission to use information has been sought by the author. Any breaches will be rectified in further editions of the book.

All rights reserved. No part of this publication may be reproduced, stored in or introduced into a retrieval system, or transmitted in any form, or by any means (electronic, mechanical, photocopying, recording or otherwise) without the prior written permission of the author. Any person who does any unauthorised act in relation to this publication may be liable to criminal prosecution and civil claims for damages. Enquiries should be made through the publisher.

Cover design: Ultimate World Publishing
Cover photo credit: GUGAI-Shutterstock.com
Layout and typesetting: Ultimate World Publishing
Editor: Marinda Wilkinson

Ultimate World Publishing
Diamond Creek,
Victoria Australia 3089
www.writeabook.com.au

CONTENTS

Dedication V
Introduction 1
Who Are You? 5
Navigation 19
Rear-view Mirror 33
Roundabouts 55
Roadblocks 65
Stalled 73
Roadmap To Success 79
Engine's Roar 89
Limitless 97
Pit Crew 107
Fly High 119
Accelerate Your Life 129
Summary 137
About the Author 139
Offer – 1 141
Offer – 2 143
Offer – 3 145

DEDICATION

F or the loves of my life Chris and Rob.

And for my grandparents Bob and Dolly, without whom this book would not exist.

We leave the womb raw, uneducated, fighting for breath, screaming our arrival into a hostile and difficult universe. Our lives are shaped by those who nurture and love us, the memories we collect both good and bad, our education and learning, our exposure to our immediate environment and the people who pass through or stay in our lives. All of it becomes a part of who we are.

This is a book for all who aspire to be more. To live a life to not just be proud of, but which is unbelievably exciting. No-one has an easy passage through life, no matter what hype they spin. We are all affected by grief, loss, disappointment, shame, emotional trauma, physical pain, hurt, deceit and distrust.

Your Last Self-Help Book is about creating a mindset which allows you to recognise negativity, analyse it, absorb it and then flip it into a positive experience. Do not allow negativity to seep in to the very fabric that is you, overwhelming you, and derailing your life journey. Eliminate it and everything else will fall into place.

Your Last Self-Help Book will show you how.

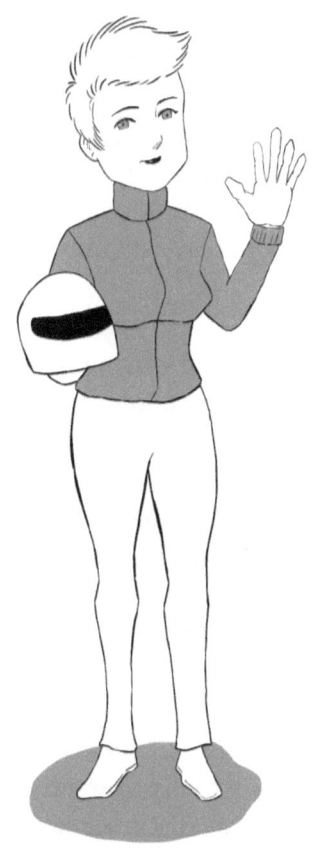

INTRODUCTION

YOUR LAST SELF-HELP BOOK

Early in 2019 I was assaulted. I had managed to reach fifty-seven years of age without anyone laying an *angry* hand on me until that day. The emotional side effects were anything but minor. The physical bruising would disappear after ten days, but qualifying the hateful actions of another person was at that point, impossible. This was one of the most challenging times in my life. It was not the assault itself which filled my mind over the months that followed, it was the hundreds of unanswered questions which invaded my daily thoughts.

Six months later I had resolved—using new techniques impressed upon me by a professional psychologist and counsellor, and old techniques which I had developed over years of dealing with life's events and difficulties—that no matter what the eventual outcome was, this person was not worth a micron more of my energy or time. The eventual decision of the courts was unimportant. Because at the end of it all, the assailants family, friends and peers would pass judgement on assaulting a woman. The sentence *they* would inflict would be well beyond anything a legal system could impose.

Up until the moment in time the assault took place, I had fully mastered and taken control of my overactive mind. Overthinking, over-analysing, creating unrealistic scenarios in my head, reliving events again and again. Anger, frustration and many more negative in-the-mind sticking points had been overcome, surpassed and filed away under done and dusted.

I was living my dream and there were no barriers I could not bypass, climb over or knock down. I was at the top of my game. No unexpected events would stand in my way. Negative people and their inherent debilitating influence were neither listened to nor engaged with. I had created my perfect bubble, built the perfect home, lived an amazing career, travelled the world, experienced unbelievable adventures, become lifelong friends with genuine and authentic like-minded people, and settled into a pattern where possibility had been fully replaced with certainty. I could flip even the most

INTRODUCTION

substantial negative experience into a positive learning platform. I had left behind circling the roundabouts of life long ago. Yet, here I was sent backwards to a place I had not visited for well over twenty years, to the merry-go-round in the mind. The place where we get stuck, endlessly rotating through the same old thoughts, unable to choose an exit in order to move on, grow, or put it down to experience and stick the event in a drawer.

I was reliving the assault over and over again, creating alternatives in my mind to the true sequence of events. Looking for answers as to why this could happen to me. Seeking out support from the witnesses who had been present. Searching for reassurance by analysing everything frame by frame. Recreating each scene but with adaptation for either a more favourable outcome, or to give the assailant some form of trauma. Succumbing to emotional reactions such as anger, shame, loss and pain. Trying to build resilience with ideas of physical retribution. I was stuck, looping around and around the roundabout, failing to see the matter for what it actually was, an unprovoked and unnecessary assault and nothing more. Instead, my mind wanted to dig deeper, to find reason where there was no real reason, to find an answer where actually there was no real question, to be able to fit the incident into a tidy drawer in my mind when in fact I had no drawer set aside for this kind of event.

It was then I was reminded about the techniques I had authored, the mindset of tools I had developed over many years which had allowed me then, now and every day to visualise my future, to make every action of every day move me closer to that future, and to eliminate the barriers which derail and stall the process.

As I often state to anyone who will listen, this is not a rehearsal—we only have one life. It is a miracle that sentient life exists at all, so don't waste a single moment of a single day on anything which holds you back or which pushes you in a direction you don't want to go in.

YOUR LAST SELF-HELP BOOK

This will be your last self-help book why? Because to live an extraordinary life, first you need to **ELIMINATE NEGATIVITY**. Once eliminated, everything else falls into place. It's not about thinking positively, it's about recognising the negative thought and flipping it into a positive action. We can repeat positive words and phrases, create affirmations and try and brainwash our mind into believing we are being the most positive person we can be. It would work just fine if our minds were conditioned to be in the positive present—except our minds prefer to work on negativity which we naturally gravitate towards. Our mind dwells on the downs of life's events not the ups. Yes, there are hundreds of people out there trying to convince you, all you need to do is think positively. But, if it were that easy our bookshelves would not be overflowing with self-help books.

After reading this book you will be able to recognise negativity quicker. You'll learn how to walk away from it and how to use tools and techniques to flip it into something else, so you can overcome it, overturn it, stamp on it or simply lock it away as it is no longer necessary.

So, shall we begin!

WHO ARE YOU?

YOUR LAST SELF-HELP BOOK

'In the egoic state, your sense of self, your identity, is derived from your thinking mind—in other words, what your mind tells you about yourself: the storyline of you, the memories, the expectations, all the thoughts that go through your head continuously and the emotions that reflect those thoughts. All those things make up your sense of self.'
Eckhart Tolle

'I am someone who can't hold on to negativity or hold on to grudges. I might feel something at a certain point, but I get tired after that. I don't carry it with me. I forgive and forget very easily, and that's the only way to be happy and peaceful.'
Deepika Padukone

You are the sum total of all of your memories and experiences. You have collected and stored everything from your life in your incredible, unique and amazing brain. Through experience and learning, you develop from a child into a fully functioning adult. Early experiences leave imprints, some of them positive, a lot of them negative. Your mind draws upon and manipulates the detail and information in your memories and uses them to determine actions, make decisions, and inform your choices. Sometimes it is our childhood experiences which lay the foundations for how we develop as adults.

The brain has incredible complexity. It controls all of the functions of the human body, every conscious and unconscious thought, action, memory, emotion and feeling. In fact, it could be classified as the most complex structure in the universe. Imagine then trying to unravel and make sense of the complexity of thoughts firing across the trillions of synapses from the hundred billion neurons within. For each connection, a synapse transmits on average one

WHO ARE YOU?

signal per second. With this kind of complexity finding where the thought begins and ends seems an insurmountable task. Perhaps it's easier to place a thought into the context of the stimuli which triggers it, for example, recognising a song, a dog barking, a crack of thunder, a needle pricking a finger, lemon juice in the mouth, a photograph in a magazine or a page in a book.

As a child of about four or five, the thoughts of bedtime brought shivers. Like most kids of that age I would kick-off at the moment going to bed was mentioned. I'm sure throughout this phase I could invent all manner of ailments and reasons to not go to bed. Regardless, I'd be sent off to the frigid sheets and the multiple lint covered woollen blankets. Then the light in the hall would be extinguished leaving only the faint light from the bottom of the stairs, where the living room door was left ajar as an early warning of me sneaking down the stairs, which I frequently did. Or at certain times of the month and depending on the weather, moonlight creeping in through the grey curtains at the window opposite my bedroom door. You see my mind had predetermined that I would be eaten by a huge tiger the moment I moved, causing the bedsheets to rustle. If I lay perfectly still in bed, arms, hands, fingers and toes all inside the covers with nothing reaching anywhere near the bed's edge, with my chin on top of the folded blanket, my head pressed firmly in the middle of the pillow, then the tiger would remain outside of the door. But, if I moved my head even slightly, the tiger would start to prowl, moving backwards and forward across the landing waiting for its cue to pounce. The tiger existed in the crack in the door. The conduit between the cold bedroom interior and the dimly lit space at the top of the stairs, the landing. If I didn't do what I was told, which was to go to sleep, the tiger would know and it would pounce and eat me up with a smack of its lips on its gleaming ivory teeth.

At some point in time one grandparent or the other had implanted this threat in a feeble attempt to deter me from leaving the warmth of the bedsheets. For the most part it worked. But, if the door was left slightly too far ajar, or the living room door was closed at the bottom of the stairs extinguishing the light then the tiger refused to appear. No tiger, no threat of being eaten, and down the stairs I would sneak, usually resulting in a clip round the ear but all the same, I got my extra bedtime story.

That is how it starts. We park the data in a vacant slot in the mind. Throughout our lives we seek out knowledge through learning and experience. All of those parking slots in one way or another contribute to who we are. Whether it is remembering what it feels like to burn a finger the only time we reach for a flame as a toddler, or how it feels to fall off a bicycle, or the stomach lifting feeling from a first kiss. Our negative learned experiences are just as important as the positive ones. It could be said that all information parked in these slots is useful, even those which we refer to as bad memories, bad feelings, negativity, doubt, pain, shame and the things we would rather forget but can't. Strangely, it appears as if these slots are conveniently sited at the forefront of the mind. Resilient memories of good times past seem all too easily to park themselves much further away from easy recall.

We are a product of our memories. Our past shapes our future as a result of the memories we capture. It is through memory that we build a world view. Through memory we build habits. When we rise in the morning we might remember that our right leg is more stable than the left, so we always put that in our trousers first. We remember when we turn on the shower, to allow it to run for a minute or two so that when we step under the shower head the water temperature has risen above sub-zero. We remember to park near the shopping trolley bay in the underground carpark, so that we have less distance to walk after completing our grocery shopping and returning the trolley to the bay. We remember how to ride a bicycle. We brush our teeth without having to think through the conscious steps. We remember how to walk. These are examples of procedural memory. The parking slots for these memories are located on what could be called the long-term floor. We don't necessarily need to think about how to do them. For

WHO ARE YOU?

example having parked in the same shopping centre and having retrieved a shopping trolley from the same bay many times, it seems as though the car almost parks itself and before we know it we're inside our favourite supermarket without hardly thinking about how we got there. The process and action of walking up to the shopping trolley, and how to retrieve it comes automatically. The more times the action is performed, the stronger the memory becomes, the easier the task is to repeat without conscious thought.

Procedural memory is a type of implicit memory, something which forms without effort. The declarative or explicit memory, however, is something which has to be consciously remembered. The time of the doctor's appointment, specific knowledge for a test, a telephone number, a birthday, the name of the manager's eldest son. Implicit is subconscious, and explicit is consciously recalled. But it doesn't end there. Episodic and semantic are the two main types of explicit (declarative) memory. Episodic are long-term memories of specific, biographical and sometimes imaginary events, such as the tiger prowling around on the bedroom landing, or the cruise ship holiday in Alaska. Semantic is the term used to cover factual memory such as names, concepts and general knowledge. Our memory is an unconscious mixture of all of the above and we are in a broad sense the product of our memories. But it does not end there. What about experiences?

Just as there are broadly two types of long-term memory, there are various types of experience with some conscious, and others unconscious. The conscious experience is the logical content, while the unconscious experience is much harder to quantify but includes emotion, feeling, belief and anticipation among others. Psychoanalysts refer to these two levels of experience as content, which captures the logic, and process which captures the feeling. Of course it isn't quite that simple, with categories covering physical, mental, emotional, spiritual, religious, social, virtual, simulation and subjective experiences.

In simple terms, we are the sum of our experiences, where experience is broadly categorised as our involvement or exposure to it.

Let's not forget the brain's notepad, short-term memory. When we say short, we mean seven items or less for ten to fifteen seconds then the items spontaneously decay. Yes, that short. We are extraordinarily clever at discarding transient unnecessary information. We might remember a phone number just long enough to get it into the contacts list on our phone. We don't need to remember it for longer, as we consciously remember it's been entered into the contacts list.

Now we have parked the memories and experiences, what about thoughts and thinking? Thoughts are broadly our ideas, beliefs and opinions about self, and the wider world around us. Our thoughts are shaped by our experiences, and often we draw on our memory in order to qualify them. Our thoughts are quite short-lived and discrete events. While we don't need to understand the neuroscience behind thought creation, it might help to know that it is the unconscious processing of the brain which brings about a conscious thought.

Thinking is the manipulation of information to problem-solve, form concepts, engage in reasoning or make decisions. As humans we have many forms of thought. Critical thinking, analysing, cognition, divergent thinking, habitual thinking, introspection, learning, memory, recollection, strategic thinking and visualisation. Then there are erroneous thoughts such as exaggeration, irrational and wishful thinking. What about emotional thinking, curiosity, empathy and rhetoric?

Thinking is something we do a lot of. If thinking always led to positive outcomes this book would never have been written. It is fair to say therefore, from this point forward, we'll be exploring why we spend so much time in our own heads thinking in the negative, and how to flip that over into a productive, positive and more rewarding approach.

WHO ARE YOU?

So, who are you? Well, it's fair to say that you are unique and probably the only person who knows who you are, is you. Or do you even know who you are?

Everyone experiences life differently. When you look at the ocean what you see is completely different to the person sitting next to you. The movement of the waves can bring back memories of a holiday, a scuba dive, snorkelling, your hatred of sand, fear of drowning, or create completely new thoughts and ideas. The person sitting next to you will be viewing the ocean in a different way. You cannot know what they are thinking, nor they know what is in your mind. You look out into the distance and remark, 'isn't it beautiful' and your partner states, 'it's boring there's nothing to look at', and you scowl at them incredulously then comment about them missing the point. Although on reflection, you don't know what the point is either, just that the view seems so serene and tranquil and brings back a buffet of positive memories. Looking at the vastness of azure blue or the cresting foaming waves brings ideas of a holiday, which instantly morphs into a cruise ship and golden beaches, a casino on the ship, bow to stern restaurants and twenty-four-hour alcohol served by twenty-somethings working their way around the world on various VISAs. Then there was the time you saw hundreds of elephant seals lounging on a beach, where was that? But there won't be enough money in the bank until that bonus arrives from the extra sales you'll make this month. Oh but that's already set aside to pay off a lump sum on the mortgage. Have we been in that house for five years already? We could sell up and move closer to the coast instead of having holidays near the ocean all of the time to get that ocean 'fix'. Although that would mean repainting the bedroom after that water leak. That'll have to go on the credit card. Perhaps we shouldn't have bought that new television. The tennis will be on tonight, wonder if they'll have it on in the pub. The lamb was really tasty last time we were there, wonder if they'll have it on the menu again although the waitress was a bit miserable, perhaps she's moved on. Does this sound familiar?

Our memories are infinite. How we recall them appears haphazard, and what we do with them once we have brought them to the forefront of our mind appears even more haphazard. Good memories which bring with them a smile are almost transient, fleeting, seemingly insignificant. Bad memories however flow more easily to the front of the queue and have more resilience. They want to remain in the present and not be pushed to their relevant parking slot somewhere at the back of the garage.

My small English junior school had a pet in every classroom. Our pet was an overfed mouse called Mickey. He was used to being handled and cuddled, cleaned out by different hands once a week and fed cheese when the teacher wasn't looking. Then one day the teacher decided Mickey should have a companion. Florence arrived the next day. Now whether at the back of the teacher's mind was an experiment in mini-mice making, or no thought given to it, Florence was not too keen on the idea of being in the same space as Mickey, and burrowed into the wood shavings as soon as she was introduced to the cage. She clearly weighed up her options over the next few days, and the very first time the cage door was opened she took a leap of faith and escaped. Florence made straight for the dead-body-sized dressing up basket and scuttled underneath it. Ms Wilson was not amused. Two of us were on hands and knees trying to see under the huge basket, which must have been the size of a commercial chest freezer, supported on fist sized casters and impossible for two small seven-year-olds to move. We could clearly see Florence underneath near the back wall, settled on her hind legs cleaning her whiskers as a cat would by licking her paws and rubbing her face. She was undeterred by a ruler, a sheet of paper or even a length of rubber piping. Ms Wilson kept asking if we'd caught her as Florence couldn't possibly be allowed to roam free throughout the school. We persevered trying to coax Florence to the front of the basket with a cube of cheese, half a dried cracker and even a slice of ham procured out of someone's lunch box but to no avail. Florence had found her freedom and no amount of encouragement would get her back into that cage. After a good thirty minutes when we

WHO ARE YOU?

should have been completing an art project, Ms Wilson, annoyed and frustrated, grabbed hold of the leather handles on the front of the basket and dragged it forward. At the same moment Florence had decided to flee and was caught underneath the moving caster. Florence was dead and her tiny head crushed. Ms Wilson heartlessly scooped Florence up in a dustpan and dropped her into the waste bin. I was mortified. Ms Wilson had extinguished a life and discarded the body without so much as a sniff or a tear.

The image of Florence, head crushed, blood and tiny brain flattened, stayed with me into my twenties. She would emerge from my memory for little reason and without warning. If only we had coaxed her out and into the cage. If only we had tried harder with the sheet of paper. Why can't people be more careful with cages? Of course animals want to escape, why do we even keep pets in cages! This morphed into why do we even keep pets? What kind of person was I to be involved in the death of an innocent animal? Clearly it was my fault, if I hadn't been there that day Florence would have lived a long life (probably the oldest mouse in history). What kind of life did Mickey have, knowing thoughtless people had murdered his companion (of three days)? The strange thing is I can't remember anything much about Mickey. Had he been removed from the classroom? Were all pets taken home after the death of Florence? Had I simply removed any thought of pets from my mind not wishing to think of their eventual demise!

In my late teens, perhaps seventeen, I was walking home from school on a colourful autumn afternoon when I came across a man kicking a dog who appeared to have defecated on the pavement. The small golden cocker spaniel cowered by the edge of the footpath its eyes wide and filled with fear. The man was not deterred by my approach and forcefully rammed his boot in the little dogs rear shouting at it as if it should understand the difference between a footpath and a road. As I drew closer I walked past a crumbling garden wall. Some of the bricks had fractured with many years of icy winter frost then summer heat. I picked up half a brick and at no more than two metres away from this man I threw it at him. It hit him squarely and with force on his wrist causing him to drop the dog lead. The little dog ran to me and I instinctively picked it up. The tirade of shouting and swearing and threats that followed would have embarrassed even the roughest tradie, but I just stood there and took the verbal abuse. While the road didn't usually have many pedestrians or passing cars at that time of day, on this day those who did happen on the scene were more than curious as to why a burly man in his forties, would be hurling abuse at a young woman in school uniform who was holding what looked to be little more than a puppy.

A large woman in a white sedan stopped her car and got out.
'What's going on?' she shouted, looking from the man to me.
'This little prick just assaulted me,' he screamed, waving his injured hand in the air which did at this point look to be broken.
She rounded the front of her car and stepped up on to the pavement and stood next to me. She lowered her voice and asked, 'what happened lovie, are you alright?'
I told her precisely what I'd seen and what I'd done. She spent a moment thinking, looking from man to dog.
'You should be ashamed of yourself kicking a defenceless little animal, what a pig.' She hurled a verbal spit ball at him.
'F&*ing keep the f&*ing dog, it's been a pain in the f&*ing arse anyway…' He unexpectedly hurled back as he turned and marched off.
Now this was quite unexpected. I'm not sure what exactly I had hoped to achieve except to stop the man from kicking the poor dog. Now I had a spaniel in my arms and I knew I was not going to be allowed to keep him, as the parental home would be forever a no pet hair environment.

'Do you want him?' I hopefully asked my saviour.
'No love I've already got two. Well, as long as you're alright.'
Almost as quickly as she'd arrived, she was in the car with a parting smile and was gone.

WHO ARE YOU?

Now what?

It was still a good twenty-minute walk to my home. I placed the little fellow on the ground and took hold of the lead. As I walked, my mind stepped through multiple scenarios. I could hide him in the garden shed. I could hide him in my bedroom, maybe even the wardrobe. I could get up each morning at about six and take him for a walk and no-one would ever know. Would he eat beans? No of course he wouldn't, I'd have to buy dog food. I was away this weekend rock climbing could he come with me? What was I going to name him? I couldn't take him to school could I? This wasn't going to end well, he'd have to go to the RSPCA. They wouldn't be able to rehome him and they'd euthanise him. He was gorgeous.

He'd stop every few metres and sniff at the grass, the pavement, a tree stump, a car wheel, some pebbles. I'd be homeless for being so foolish. What a stupid thing to do throwing a brick at a grown man, I could have broken his arm. I'd get home and the police would be on the doorstep. I'd be in prison if someone saw me with the dog. How could I get him into the house without being seen? I could leave him tied up in the yard then walk to the front as usual. Would he smell? How much water would he drink?

The man was never seen again. I gave a description to the police but neither he nor the woman in the white sedan were identified. Our next-door neighbour eagerly took 'Buster' in for fostering and with no owners found, long before microchipping or mandatory identification or licensing, that is where he stayed with an older spaniel called Copper until he died peacefully in his sleep at eighteen years of age.

I was not charged with anything, although the local police officer who lived around the corner from my home, gave me a stern talking to about prison cells and lifelong police records had the man come forward. Did the death of an innocent mouse have a role to play? Certainly my childhood was filled to the brim with David Attenborough, exotic animals and a strong sense of animal justice.

YOUR LAST SELF-HELP BOOK

The memory has troubled me for many years. I should recall the beautiful innocent and grateful face of Buster who greeted me with effervescent tail wagging every time I walked into the neighbour's house for a five-minute play. I should recall the softness of his tiny muzzle and his teddy bear paws. I should recall the exuberance, or the exhilaration of the confrontation. But I don't. I see the man collecting a brick and hurling it at me, splitting open my skull. I see him punching me and beating me as I lay on the ground. I see Buster dead on the pavement.

It is these images fake and untrue which would crowd my mind at unexpected times. The reality of the event almost lost and shrouded as if the falsehoods were far more enticing, more alluring, more enjoyable to recall. Pathetic really. The true and real account is uplifting, dangerous, accomplished, brave, adventurous and is actually much more indicative of my personality. Yet still my mind tried to conjure the alternatives.

I have carried the love of all animals through my life. I can't bear to see an animal in pain, suffering or ill. As I've grown older I can no longer bear to watch animal documentaries and the reality of the hunt. A news item which showed the suffering of overheated sheep on a live export ship resulted in the channel being instantly changed. I don't want those images in my mind to reappear when I least expect them. I can hear the news story and take on board the content and be determined to end live export because after all, if boxed frozen meat were more lucrative and earned greater profit, it would take precedence and prison ships would not exist.

These events and many dozens of other experiences, memories and learning are what has shaped me as a person. This is how I have arrived at where I now am. This is who I am. Do you know who you are?

WHO ARE YOU?

Take time now to think about three distinct childhood experiences. If they don't come instantly to mind don't dig. How about things you liked or disliked doing, such as visiting someone, school, places, activities or sport?

- Why do these experiences stand out in your mind?
- Is each one broadly remembered as positive or negative?
- How have these experiences shaped who you are?

NAVIGATION

YOUR LAST SELF-HELP BOOK

'Common sense would suggest that having ability, like being smart, inspires confidence. It does, but only while the going is easy. The deciding factor in life is how you handle setbacks and challenges. People with a growth mindset welcome setbacks with open arms.'

Travis Bradberry

'Sometimes in life, when bad things happen to us, or things aren't going our way, or we're faced with a challenge or a problem, it's how you look at the problem; it's how you do it to change your mindset, to dilute the negativity.'

Alesha Dixon

How you navigate life's challenges, can tell you a great deal about yourself. What you believe about yourself can impact your successes and your failures. If you believe you were born with certain qualities which have ultimately formed your personality and they are unchangeable, then you most likely have a fixed mindset. If however, you believe your qualities and abilities develop, change or are strengthened through experience, then you most likely have a growth mindset. Recognising growth affords a greater ability to navigate your own mind and use the experiences and challenges you encounter to evolve your thinking and challenge your beliefs.

Less than a week out from the first court hearing for the assault my mind shifted into overdrive. My brain was trying to process numerous outcomes while working on various scenarios. Pleading guilty, not guilty. When I would next have to endure this person's presence in the work environment and how I would handle it. My husband would be in court, but what if the accused chose to send the lawyer to court while he would attend work instead, putting him in relative close proximity to me? This would be an intentional emotional challenge. If he pleaded guilty then what? Could I have him removed from the workplace there and then? Why hadn't that already been done? Why had the predominately male senior staff not done something to remove this person? Anyone and everyone could be a target. There was no way to predict the original incident so how could anyone be certain a new trigger would not elicit a second?

Now my nights were sleepless. I was wide awake running over the same pointless scenarios. Reliving the event in minute detail. I tried to picture clothing worn on the day. Where everyone had been sitting. Which desks were occupied by which staff. Was it sunny or raining? What would be important information? This was destructive negativity. The balance and stability of my emotional position which I had spent so many years achieving and maintaining, lay as wreckage at my feet. Any self-worth or value I brought to the workplace had been wiped out. Now I was just another statistic, one of the many people bullied in the workplace, of women shamed by the actions of a man, caught in a system which favours the accused. Innocent until 'proven' guilty. With five full days to go before his first court appearance, how was I going to get off this roundabout?

In the pitch black of night, the dog snoring at the foot of the bed, and the wind howling its way around the house roof and nearby trees I purposefully listened to those sounds and tried to focus my eyes out of the window, looking into the blackness of the night.

There wasn't anything to count. As a child and young adult my coping mechanism was to count things. I'd count paving stones, bricks in the wall, circles on the wallpaper, lines on the vinyl flooring, tiles in the bathroom, people's heads on the train, seats, markings on the road, yellow cars, sheep in the paddock, fence posts, squares on the games board, anything and everything rather than allow my mind to deal with the problem or issue at hand. I could block out resentment or negative thoughts but it was not a productive resolution and I would always return to them at a later date.

YOUR LAST SELF-HELP BOOK

There are moments and events in our lives which we can never pigeon hole and move on from. Around 1994, I was midway through undergraduate studies at university, having returned to learning after not getting too far in project management within a government role. At the time, I had a young son to feed, clothe and provide for, when I experienced one of those earth-shattering unexpected, unforeseeable life-changing events.

A lecturer was absent without leave and the students were not told of this until a few minutes before the lecture was due to start. As there was nothing else on the timetable for the afternoon, and the weather was miserable and grey, I drove the thirty minutes to home. To my surprise my partner was home. I bounded up the stairs excited to share an unusually free afternoon and found him cowering in the wardrobe. He was wearing only his underwear and refused to get to his feet claiming that he didn't want me to look at him. I was puzzled, perplexed, confused—in fact almost hysterical. The man I'd known for close to five years was on his knees in a dark wardrobe refusing to get up or look at me. I can't remember what was running through my mind. I would discover two hours later that he couldn't face me because he was wearing lipstick and mascara, and had spent his lunch hour patrolling the neighbourhood in women's clothes.

I sat on the lounge, knees together, sober, staring into space. I was living with a cross-dresser and never so much as suspected it. My mind was trying to process this information. I recalled the evening I returned home after a few days working away. Unpacking in the bedroom, I noticed fragments of a condom on the carpeted floor. I believed the pleading commentary that he was not having an affair and it was something else entirely, although at the time he refused to tell me what that something else was. Now it came flooding out. The condoms had been filled with water and pushed into a bra he was wearing, and one had burst.

I didn't know this man at all. Behind all of the subterfuge and lies were the fragments of a relationship. Everyone deserves a second chance he would later plead, I promise to never do it again, as bin bags filled with makeup and women's clothes were discarded into the communal garbage area of the apartment block in which we lived. Except now the rules had changed, now there was no trust at all on my part, and this brought with it a heightened sense of awareness. I instinctively checked the garbage area the morning of the weekly collection, to find the bags had been removed and the contents returned to the hidden store under the floorboards. Of course I'd checked the wardrobe while he was at work, returning home instead of going to university, hiding like a criminal in the nearby pub car park until his van drove past, heart thumping in my ears, my mind a storm of anger and shame. I mean, why would a man be crouching in a wardrobe unless there was something to hide in there? It had taken me all of two minutes to observe and work out that the shoes were never in the same place twice and to rip back the loosely laid carpet to find a crudely cut square in the flooring with a finger hole drilled into it for easy removal. Inside, there were the bin bags. I thought about throwing it all out of the window onto the lawn but the neighbours would probably assume it was mine, the discarded debris of yet another recent argument.

The relationship, if it can be called that, continued for another few years. I had gone from undergraduate studies to postgraduate studies. I was struggling with a complex statistics assignment and had spent too much time in the student bar one afternoon. I jumped in the car and set off to drive home knowing I was well over the legal alcohol limit. It was winter and the road was icy and shining in the darkness. Where I should have turned off the highway I just continued on, gradually pressing my foot forward on the accelerator, taking the car from a legal speed to well over two hundred kilometres per hour. I was in the second lane of a four-lane wide southbound motorway. Between my legs was an open bottle of whisky from which I took a good long mouthful. It burnt its way down my throat forcing me to close my eyes and wince. I gripped the bottle with my thighs and removed my hands from the steering wheel. I kept my eyes tightly shut. The car was still accelerating and I could feel a slight judder from the wheels. I was surrounded by what seemed like complete silence. I could feel nothing either physically or emotionally. The image which unexpectedly came into my mind was my son's smiling face.

The car had covered a good mile under no physical control and travelling at ludicrous speeds on a normally busy stretch of motorway. I opened my eyes to see I was almost at the junction which led to my ex-husband's parent's house, where my son was staying overnight. I just caught the slip road and veered the car off at high speed. Fortunately it was a long descent to the roundabout at the bottom. I didn't turn right towards him but left into a service station car park. I parked the car well away from everyone else and got out of the car and was violently ill. I emptied the rest of the whisky onto the grass but kept the bottle. I would later glue a photograph of my son aged ten over the label, add a lampshade and light fitment to it and used it for many years as a desk light and constant reminder. The car had stayed in the second lane, and everyone else in surrounding vehicles whoever they had been had found their way safely to their destination that night. I woke up the next morning freezing cold. The ends of my fingers were blue and I felt so sick all I could do was wretch stomach acid all over the steering wheel.

The images, the thoughts, the regret, the self-loathing which would revisit me every other day I would qualify a few years later as the **EVOLUTIONARY MOMENT**, the point where I pivoted from negative to positive. Why? Because I recognised my own self-pity and **ACTIVATED CHANGE**.

Of course removing myself from the relationship was not that easy with threats of self-harm hurled at me, then the emotional *I don't need you because I'm having sex with this person* angle, and many more attempts to prevent my exit. It was messy and not as simple as I might suggest but it resulted in a new career direction, working for an American company of worldwide renown and reputation.

NAVIGATION

I now found myself in a whole different sphere. I was immediately immersed in a supportive, almost family-like working environment where employee counselling and therapy of one form or another was normal—in fact, it was actively encouraged and paid for as part of the compensation package. I had also been transported to another part of the country and eventually oversees. This helped to cut old ties. At this point I was only seeing my son once per fortnight due to the distance and constant oversees travel but my career went into overdrive with quick and stellar success.

How I was now interacting with my past had changed. My upbringing, my experiences had not always been negative but my way of seeing them had not been positive either. As is often said, it is not the good times we remember most vividly, it is the bad. If all we dwell on are the negative events then how we see things, will also be tinged in negativity. Plus, of course, we need to ask ourselves, what exactly is negative about it? Why is my immediate reaction to turn to the dark side of the event? Is there anything positive to be seen in it? Yes I know, easier said than done.

My father left my mother when I was two years old. He was a Canadian engineer on a five-year contract in Cambridgeshire and when his time was up he had to return to Toronto. My mother chose to resist this and ended up in a bitter divorce. The outcome was that my grandparents took control of parenting. A lot of my early years are missing from my memory. Optimistically I could reflect on that as a positive outcome, given had they been sad or horrid years then no doubt I would remember them in greater detail. I do remember the tiger on the landing, and the shotgun kept in the pendulum case of the grandmother clock at the bottom of the stairs. I remember the overgrown back garden of the reclusive neighbour next door and the occasional visits from his grandson. I remember my holidays were always to the same place often numerous times each year, where the bed and breakfast overlooked an enchanted castle frequented by knights and distressed damsels, with a dragon living on top of the keep.

YOUR LAST SELF-HELP BOOK

I remember dawn walks with my grandfather scouring the landscape for field mushrooms, or to shoot the occasional hare. I remember the never-ending supply of books, of plain paper exercise books and coloured pencils. I remember pressing dried flowers into my grandmother's leather-bound book. I remember using oils and cotton wool to polish coins brought at lunch times by the insurance man, who would empty his leather saddle bag onto the kitchen table and drink tea, while my grandmother fingered the change for a date that was missing from her collection. I remember homegrown green tomatoes ripening on the kitchen window sill, or brown crabs being dropped into boiling water on the huge cast iron range. I remember Whisky the black and white collie dog, abandoned by my mother at the same time that she abandoned me, being allowed into the house to sleep in front of the range when the winter nights were howling with wind and blasting the roof with hail and snow. I remember being taken to the hospital after being run over by a motorbike, and remember the pain from my swollen cheek around the five stitches near my right ear. I remember my next visit to a hospital where I was forced to wait outside the private room door because my mother was visiting my grandmother inside. After ten minutes the door burst open and my mother who I hardly knew, flung herself dramatically outwards. She grabbed on to a passing nurse and screamed 'my mother is dying from cancer of the stomach'. She then looked down at me with a contorted, twisted and pained look of sudden realisation, and spat at me 'don't expect me to look after you'.

My grandmother died eight months later. I was being prepared for transition in the weeks and months leading up to her passing. It started with an overnight stay at my mother's new flat. I have no idea where she was living before that for the eleven years I had hardly seen her. I had no idea what she had done for a living except for the occasional visit to a bakery where she served behind the counter, and then there had been talk of her training to be a psychiatric nurse. One night per week became two and then three. It was a frigid upstairs flat without heating or an inside bathroom. I hated it. A

NAVIGATION

month into this routine my grandparents relocated from the three-bedroom house I'd spent all of my time in, to a smaller two-bedroom council house nearer to my mother. My grandmother started to go to church and I was tasked with accompanying her because as my mother said, 'you have to go because I couldn't possibly go into a church!'. Within three months I was up to five nights per week at my mother's flat with visits from my grandmother every other day for tea. She started to bring her own towel which she laid across the armchair seat cushion and as she sat down she would lift up her skirt so that her bare bottom would be on the towel. Something was clearly very wrong but I was taught to be respectful, and in this instance it was respectful to not ask too many questions. The towel was always stained when she stood up to leave. Then, without warning in the middle of the night she was gone. We didn't have a telephone in the house, we had only just invested in a television, and there had been no knock on the door—I just knew.

I can roughly pinpoint the day when the emotional abuse started some six months after my grandmother's death. Forced to become a parent against her will this was all going to be my fault. I was, I learned, a mistake. I was the result of a career-ending unplanned pregnancy. In fact, had I not been born, clearly the marriage would have continued, and she would have been some country Canadian wife playing golf at the weekends and fully immersed in *ladies who lunch* during the week. Instead, she was now forced to return to college to get some basic qualifications and then go on to join the tax office. Clearly, this was not how she had planned her life. Having said that she did eventually retire close to fifty-five years of age, with a pension equivalent to seventy-five percent of her salary, index linked to inflation and any future government pay rises. By the time she died in 2015 aged only seventy-six, she had not long returned from her thirty-second cruise. She died alone, discovered only by chance after my son raised growing concerns over her mental and physical wellbeing with her local doctors' surgery.

YOUR LAST SELF-HELP BOOK

I was twelve when my grandmother died and twenty when my grandfather died. To me he was never the same after my grandmother's death. How do people truly cope with the loss of their only love? I was first married at nineteen to a man I couldn't stand. On my wedding day my mother asked if I wanted to change my mind. I replied with the suitable response that I could always get a divorce. My grandfather died the following year. I spent more time away from my marriage than actively engaged in it, employed as a ski and outdoor activities instructor floating around the UK and Europe. In 1985 my son was born and a year later divorce proceedings were started. The downside of this was putting myself in the very real position of being homeless. I wrote to a women's charity asking, no pleading for help. The council had stated they would not offer me housing unless I was physically on the street, and then more than likely it would be bed and breakfast accommodation not long-term housing. I was out of a destructive marriage which I'd only got into as a method of getting away from my mother, with a one-year-old to look after.

Once I had settled into my own home, the charity offered childcare in the form of babysitting services. I started working in fast food at weekends, while my ex-husband had mandatory visits to my son. I had a stint in a car manufacturer's canteen on nightshifts, then progressed to car sales before I finally got a break with a government job. It was a project management role in the education department. But as a project officer working in finance, I wasn't going anywhere fast anytime soon.

I was now in a relationship with a closet cross-dresser and trying to maintain my sanity by jumping willingly out of aircraft once a fortnight, while my son was staying with my ex-husband's parents. I eventually threw in the towel with the government and applied to university. You know most of the rest. While in the closet relationship (literally), I somehow ended up being the breadwinner, he having been burned by his previous relationship when (he claimed) his ex-wife stripped him of his businesses, money and any chance of custody of their son. Irony can be so harsh. Once I left him he turned his life around and became a millionaire property dealer.

I carried the negativity of this history and timeline around with me like an albatross. I remember I had very little positivity. I would look for things, no, wait for things to go wrong. So I did a lot of drinking. In fact I'd go so far as to say I must have been very close to being an alcoholic; but then I'd started drinking at thirteen. Well yes, I suppose we might as well complete the picture.

After junior school (infants, juniors and seniors in the United Kingdom back then) I passed all of the tests for grammar school which I joined in 1973. A year in, my grandmother died and I had some time off, although how that came about I'm not sure. On my return the headmaster, a very well-respected man, put me in the hands of a mentor, to help me through this troubling period. He was my history teacher and I'm guessing he was not long out of teacher training college and was approximately twenty-five or six. Within six months he had started to sexually abuse me. This didn't actually go on for long, perhaps a year. It had stopped before my thirteenth birthday, and before I started my first period. Perhaps that was part of his modus operandi. My first year was the only year of the seven spent at grammar school where I was a student in his history class. I do believe the French teacher, whose classroom was opposite, had some suspicion of this extra-curricular activity as she stopped me one day in the corridor on my way to geography, and asked if there was anything I would like to tell her. I hesitated for far too long but in the end, with his 'who is going to believe you anyway' threat ringing in my ears, I smiled and walked past her.

Once my period started I was inducted into the Saturday night party club (yes aged thirteen), where once a month we'd all truck round to each other's houses for a teenage party. We only visited my place once because the rules were far too strict and no alcohol was allowed, which was completely unacceptable to my friends. Every other parent however would happily buy bottles of cheap sweet cider and the occasional box of beer. Yes, thirteen. The parties got thinner as we reached exam age but once we'd all sailed through those and entered sixth form then the show really took off. Now we were in an elite club where the male teachers took part. Every couple of months we'd be away for the weekend rock climbing or canoeing at outdoor centres. We were all between sixteen and eighteen by then so the alcohol was more acceptable. My mother encouraged my absences and always gave me a generous allowance. I would later work out that she had something going with a work colleague who she would eventually marry, and having a nosey sixteen-year-old around the house spoilt the fun. Having said that my stepfather was a wonderful, wonderful man. Much to my surprise their marriage lasted, although I suspect that was more as a result of my stepfather's balanced and forgiving personality.

In order to navigate your mind and your thoughts, you must first confront your memories. I went through a stage where I tried to metaphorically put my fingers in my ears and sing lalala to myself to block it all out. It didn't work. Supressing the past is not the solution.

Do you know yourself? This is where the journey begins. It isn't enough to live in the moment, to meditate and clear the mind, because doing either of those is impossible if you have not recognised, accepted, set aside or sent backwards, all of those images and thoughts which destructively invade your mind when you least expect them to. Confront and accept your memories.

Oh and by the way, this is not where the story ends. But remember, the key was the **EVOLUTIONARY MOMENT** which **ACTIVATED CHANGE**. That is not to say negative and gut-wrenching events didn't happen after that—they did. I just had a greater capacity to deal with them, and the wisdom to move more easily past the roadblocks, and get off the roundabouts.

Do you believe you were born with certain qualities which have ultimately formed your personality, and that they are unchangeable?

NAVIGATION

Or do you believe your qualities and abilities develop, change or are strengthened through experience? The former indicates a fixed mindset while the latter, a growth mindset. There is no right or wrong answer however, those who lean towards growth are more likely to recognise their evolutionary moment and take charge of activating change. Those who lean towards having fixed qualities would need help pinpointing an evolutionary moment.

List three **EVOLUTIONARY MOMENTS**. These are moments in your life which **ACTIVATED CHANGE** or **ACTIVATED GROWTH**.

- Did you activate change or growth for each evolutionary moment?
- Was the change or growth positive or negative?
- How did you change or grow as a result of each moment?

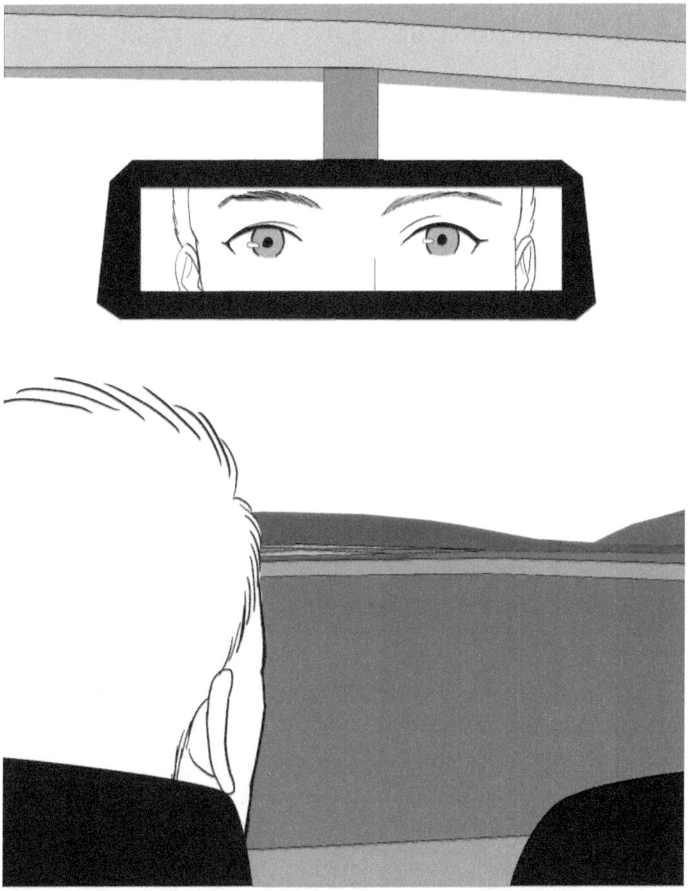

REAR–VIEW MIRROR

'I do believe in the old saying, "What does not kill you makes you stronger". Our experiences, good and bad, make us who we are. By overcoming difficulties, we gain strength and maturity.'

Angelina Jolie

'I spent a lot of years trying to outrun or outsmart vulnerability by making things certain and definite, black and white, good and bad. My inability to lean into the discomfort of vulnerability limited the fullness of those important experiences that are wrought with uncertainty: Love, belonging, trust, joy, and creativity to name a few.'

Brené Brown

Life is not just about what we experience, but *how* we experience it and our lasting memory of the experience. Collectively those experiences, along with knowledge, shape us as human beings. I've given experience three broad categories. The road crash, the middle of the road, and the ultimate road trip. You may want to create your own, or expand on the three.

Road crash experiences

First, let's look at what we could call our road crash experiences, remembering not all bad experiences sink their teeth into our long-term memory. Also remembering what is mediocre for one, may be devastating for someone else. Many bad experiences fade because their impact is temporary or transient. As women we may want children. As the old saying goes, if we truly remembered the pain of childbirth, we'd never have another child. The pain of giving birth can be *fairly* classified as a bad experience, but as a memory, it doesn't really hang around. Yes we remember it was painful, but we don't actually store away the details of the physical pain.

As an exuberant ski instructor some eighteen months after taking up a role in the Italian Alps, participating in the parade of light where resort owners and ski instructors formed a decorative line zig-zagging down the main resort ski run holding lanterns, I skied into a tree trying to avoid a toddler running across the run. It was painful to say the least as my right knee took the full force of impact. The knee was swollen for weeks but the leg wasn't broken so I carried on working. If the pain seemed worse on any particular day I'd massage it and numb the brain by drinking copious amounts of mulled wine in the evenings. Not paying attention to my body, not listening to my common sense, and probably not having the wisdom or experience to realise I was doing far more damage to the leg than had I rested it for a month meant the next time I hit a tree, which was as a result of losing control after taking a jump, ended in a difficult and almost career-ending double fracture.

I hobbled around on half pay for a good six weeks helping out with washing up and waxing skis and then happily returned to the slopes. My experience was severe enough to put me off taking high jumps, but not so serious it put me off skiing altogether. Neither the accident nor the recovery put me off alcohol. Could I remember the pain of the break? No, but I could remember the inconvenience and financial pressure of not being able to instruct. It was not the memory of the pain which made me more cautious, it was remembering the financial hardship.

We remember what it's like to have to deal with a puncture to the car tyre on the side of the road in the pouring rain, but it doesn't stop us jumping in the car every morning to drive to work. In our memories are the procedural steps for safely removing the wheel, locating the spare and attaching it to the car, but there is little emotional trauma as a result of our actions. Unless of course the circumstances are such that unforeseen or unpredictable additional events result from the puncture. For example a failure to ensure the car won't roll forward or backwards once the car has been jacked up. Or another car stops, two men jump out, run over to you and demand your wallet. The addition of the unexpected, could impact how you might deal with a puncture in the future. You may be less likely to handle the wheel change yourself and more inclined to lock the car doors and call the roadside recovery service you always ensure is paid for with membership fully up to date. Perhaps you've never experienced changing a car tyre because you have assumed you can't do it, or decided you don't want to experience how to do it. You haven't committed the actions to your memory, you've committed the decision of inaction instead.

As a group of instructors working for an outdoor centre in a city in the United Kingdom, we collectively decided to have a weekend away. It was of course a busman's holiday involving skiing, sailing, climbing mountains and spending too much time in various bars. On our second day, with heavy snow falling and every one of us with hangovers, we were gingerly driving up a steep farm track to Keswick's (then) only winter ski runs. Nearing the top of the track we came across two cars who had collided after sliding on compacted snow and ice. We all piled out of our hired minibus into what seemed like complete silence. The snowfall was so heavy it almost turned the early morning into early evening. Instinct and training would take over. We split into two groups to deal with each car. We were all instructors and all well-trained in first aid. The car I attended had two unconscious passengers, a man and a woman. The driver a man, had his head slumped forward with pink foam exuding from his nose and clear difficulty breathing. This happened in the days long before airbags. The windscreen was shattered. He had a huge flap of skin and hair folded back from his forehead and scalp revealing his blood-stained skull. He would regain consciousness first. There was no way to tell if he had damage to his spine in this position but without intervention he would surely suffocate. Carefully, with one person in the back seat holding his shoulders in place, his chin was lifted off his chest so that his airway could open. Almost immediately he opened his eyes. He appeared to have no idea where he was but his eyes revealed fear. While others checked the cars were safe with no immediate danger from leaking fuels, and with stones and lumps of wood chocking the wheels of the second car which was at risk of rolling down the hill, we methodically worked to assess all casualties. It was also in the days when huge Velcro straps were favoured instead of triangular bandages to immobilise limbs. The emergency services were called but were twenty minutes away due to the isolation of the location. We could not risk moving this driver for fear he had sustained spinal damage, so one of our team held him firmly upright against his seat, while I folded the huge flap of skin forward so I could get a bandage over his head and down and around under his chin. At this point his wife who was his passenger regained consciousness, and informed us that the other car had been coming towards them and appeared to have lost control and hit them head-on. She had no idea of speed but said both cars were travelling slower than normal due to the snow on the road. The windscreen had shattered, after that they must have blacked out. She appeared to be alright but we wanted her to stay in the car to reassure her husband who was certainly not alright. With reassurance and smiling faces we were for all intents and purposes just treading water until the emergency services arrived, at which point we handed over to them.

Training is one thing, having to put that training into practice is something else. The theory is nothing like the reality and what is not learned in the classroom, is how a stressful situation will affect each individual. What is missing from a simulation, is adrenalin and situation. Each situation will be different, and everyone's adrenalin levels affect their body in different ways. Some are better able to cope with the surges of adrenalin while others attending to help, can often feel similar effects to the person involved in the accident or event. The accident victim will experience the effects of physical shock; the first responder and the accident victim will experience the effects of emotional shock sometime later.

Emotional shock has no clinical diagnosis, but is a term commonly used by mental health professionals. The effects of emotional shock can be short-lived, or last a lifetime. Studies of the amygdala, which is central to the brain's stress response, does indicate some people are more susceptible to the effects of stress than others. Those with high amygdala activity tend to back away from high-risk activities and will be more cautious so, when involved in a traumatic and stressful event, they may feel the effects more strongly than someone who regularly jumps out of an aircraft for fun.

One of our group was fairly new to instructing. An accomplished rock climber and mountaineer there were no outward signs, especially given her high-risk chosen sport, that she would be susceptible to stress. While attending the accident, she had been at the passenger side of the vehicle I was tending to. She was comforting the passenger, chattering away, trying to deflect attention away from her seriously injured husband, and doing an amazing job. On a Monday a month after the accident, she didn't turn up for work. In those days it was a landline phone call or a knock on the door to get hold of someone. Neither resulted in contact. Another month went by and we still had no idea where she was or what had happened. Eventually a letter of resignation arrived which had been written by her father. She was in France on a climbing expedition. She wouldn't be returning to work. She would never again be an instructor and had decided to return to university to follow a career in microbiology. It would be another two years before information would filter through from friends of friends of family members that she had attempted to take her own life with a prescription drug overdose. The trauma of the accident, the blood, the close proximity and very real possibility of witnessing death, the smell, the cold, in her eyes the horror, had all culminated in a call for help. Thankfully her father came home early from work that day and then family support took over to see her emerge from the other side of her darkness.

I look at my road crash experiences as an incident, event, occurrence, which promoted change in me at a fundamental level. Something so negative it causes a paradigm shift in behaviour, beliefs, emotions or personality. Usually, we don't collect too many of these. Hopefully, they can be counted on one hand. In my life I consider being sexually abused, the death of my grandfather, *almost* being left homeless (and I do stress the word almost), discovering that my second partner was a cross-dresser, the sudden death of my third partner, and being physically assaulted, as my road crash experiences. It is these experiences which become **EVOLUTIONARY MOMENTS** because they **ACTIVATE CHANGE**.

With hindsight I would never have married my first husband. I was far too young, had little real experience of life, and was doing it for all of the wrong reasons. The divorce was more of a relief than a turning point, suddenly finding myself with a one-year-old and nowhere to live, was something else entirely. My mother of course did not come to my rescue with the offer of my old bedroom, even on a temporary basis. Only then, did I realise just how negative my relationship with her had actually always been. The true reality of being without the relative security of four walls and a roof was much more devastating. Sitting behind this in my mind was an inability to reconcile why my mother would not offer me shelter. This would churn around in my mind for years and years. In fact it had such an impact on my mental health, combined with many, many other incidents and negative encounters with her, that when my son reached aged three, I effectively closed the door and did not speak to her for the next eight years.

Only four years into the relationship, my third partner suddenly died of heart failure. It was January 2001, an extraordinary year on so many levels. I had resolved, post cross-dresser, not to step too quickly into any kind of permanent relationship. Less than a year later, that resolution had been thrown out of the window.

I first met John some ten years earlier as we were both studying for a Diploma in Training Management. Fast forward to 1996. I was at a conference in Edinburgh, Scotland and he was delivering a keynote presentation on the challenges of developing training plans for offshore oil and gas workers. We kept in touch by phone and email with conversations dominated by change management and information technology. We had no idea we were both actually based in the same city, Aberdeen.

By the year 2000 when the computing world was trying to recover from its oversell of the concept of world ending scenarios resulting from the changeover from 1999 to 2000, I had been offered a senior lecturer role at a main university. This involved relocating from Scotland to middle England, but gave both of us the opportunity to grow, and to find a home together. Six months after completing the house purchase, on 31 January 2001, John died. I had delivered him to the local railway station that morning. He had an interview for a senior executive role with one of the country's leading industry boards. He had just taken his seat before the interview panel and was being introduced when he lifted his right hand gently to his chest, closed his eyes, slid off the chair and died. Paramedics worked for hours, transferring him to a main London hospital, but with no success.

Three months later I would return to work to awkward conversations and a reduced workload. This road crash experience would sharpen my life perspective. After all, if a seemingly healthy human being can suddenly die with no apparent precursor or warning, no-one can class themselves immune from the same.

For the first month after John died I barely got out of bed and when I did I lay on the couch with the television on. The curtains remained closed and I didn't answer the phone to anyone except my son and my closest friends. Every few weeks Linda my wonderful, wonderful friend would come around and cook Sunday lunch. I was self-absorbed and drowning in self-pity.

The second month was spent out on my motorbike. Both John and I were avid sports bike riders, running up and down the country at weekends to visit family and spending copious amounts of our earnings on motorbike accessories, touring holidays and new bikes. My Honda CBR600 gave me freedom, fresh clean air and the opportunity to visit a new café every day. The reason for riding my motorbike as often as possible was to close my mind off to invasive negative thoughts and memories. South Yorkshire and Derbyshire in England are home to some of the most challenging, testing and twisting roads. They are every motorbike rider's dream. Never-ending rolling from side to side trying to increase cornering speed over multiple runs. The concentration needed to make a controlled and fast run along these roads is immense. Motorbike riding became a completely immersive activity. I could guarantee I could ride my favourite roads and never have to think about anything other than the run into the very next corner, then the next, and the next. A month of this gave my mind a vacation from itself.

My evenings of the third month were filled with reading and planning my first trip to Australia with my son. Overnight was the worst. Keeping the demons and memories out of my mind was harder once underneath the bedsheets. I would leave my television on the all-night news. I had to concentrate on the words being spoken by the newsreader. I was determined to not think about John because remembering was so destructive. I would have the occasional relapse and night of uncontrolled sobbing but I'd rush the next morning to get out on the motorbike. It was frigid cold and often pouring with rain or snowing but I still went out. I began writing a fiction book. It wasn't particularly good, was cliched and predictable, but it occupied my mind. I was cleared by my doctor to return work on 30 April.

At the end of June that year I was knocked off my motorbike by a minibus whose driver had seen the entrance to the golf club, and turned across the road right in front of me to enter it. She would later claim that the main right pillar of the windscreen on the front of the bus completely masked me from her view, a claim which would be supported by the investigating police. When I regained consciousness it seemed everything on my left side was painful. My left collarbone and wrist were broken and my bike lay shattered and crumpled and was close to a total write-off.

Middle of the road experiences

I had a new resilience—this was not a metaphorical road crash experience, this was a middle of the road life experience. I can barely remember it now, in fact I would hardly remember it at all were it not for the fact that the collarbone has never knitted back together. One bone grinds and catches the other occasionally causing discomfort but it has no true pain. I was back at work the same week. The worst part of the entire experience was not being able to ride the bike, which was taken for a full insurance rebuild. I remember the day I jumped back on it three months later with crystal clear iced water clarity. I remember the transit van it turned up in. The bearded and tattooed young driver who wheeled it out down the ramp. I remember him starting it up and with a massive grin he asked me if I'd missed it! I remember getting into my bike kit and jumping on it almost immediately. I remember my legs were like jelly trying to three point it in my dead-end street. I remember riding it sixty miles to a well-known pub frequented by sports bike riders. The memory of the accident however is muddied and unimportant.

The accident while painful did not impact my ability or desire to ride. It is broadly classified as a negative event—after all, it was a road accident which had a very real impact on my ability to drive to work, days off work, ability to write (being left-handed), medical appointments with specialists to try and re-knit the bones together, and the underlying thought that the minibus driver may not have been fully insured. The marked difference between road crash experiences and middle of the road experiences are the depth of the retained memories. Of course this is not true for everyone who would consider any kind of road accident a literal road crash experience.

REAR-VIEW MIRROR

Middle of the road experiences enter long-term memory, but the parking slot they are assigned to can be overwritten at any point. We have to dig deep and ferret around in the mind to try and recover the detail. We can remember some of the content but not necessarily everything. My association with my bike was more personal so of course I remember it was painted matt black with orange decals. I have absolutely no memory of the minibus except it might have been white.

In 2005 I was on a skiing holiday in France when on the second day an out of control snowboarder slammed into the lift queue bowling most of the skiers over like skittles. One person had to be helicoptered off the slope, another had a broken wrist but could stand, while I was wheeled to a waiting ambulance with a suspected torn anterior cruciate ligament of the left knee. I spent the rest of the week in the hotel bedroom bored out of my brain. The insurance company would not fly us home early due to the likelihood of deep vein thrombosis and dislodged clots. I remember this middle of the road experience more for the annoyance factor than for its long-term impact. I remember not being able to interpret the ambulance driver's French or understand he was stating he would not transfer me to the clinic in the adjoining ski village until he had two-hundred Euros in his hand. I didn't have a clue what he was saying and it took two other skiers to relay the bad news. Mobile phones were a valuable resource in those days, so I phoned my then fiancé to ask him to meet the ambulance at the bottom of the main run with the cash. The whole scene resembled a drug deal. At the clinic the doctor's English was much better. He could tell by manipulation of the knee that the ligament was badly damaged or torn and said I had to return to the clinic every day for a week for an anti-clotting injection, at a cost of two-hundred Euros for the transfer and another hundred Euros for the injection. I looked at him incredulously. He could see the disgust on my face and added something about having no alternative option unless I was able to inject myself. I quickly told him I had plenty of experience being able to self-inject, at which point his face curled into a grin. I couldn't be bothered to explain that during pregnancy I was diagnosed with diabetes (which never went away) and had to inject insulin as a result, but allowed him to muse over his interpretation that I probably had a heroin addiction. I thanked him for his prescription for syringes and something along the lines of heparin and heavy-duty pain killers, and spent the rest of the week drugged up to the eyeballs soaking in après ski alcohol. My fiancé was not impressed although his schoolboy French was way better than mine, which at least meant he could make himself understood in the supermarket otherwise we may have starved to death in the first few days.

The swelling reduced after three days and I was able to hobble around the resort. The insurance company were incredible. They transferred me by private ambulance to Geneva and paid for a full line of four seats at the front of the plane so I could keep the injured leg elevated. My memories of annoyance didn't end there. More time off work for assessment with the local hospital consultant who was not convinced I had torn anything. Two sets of MRI scans later and I was sent for extensive physiotherapy. The report would read that I was 'tentative' during my exercises. After three months I was signed off, I assumed awaiting surgery. It was a very strange injury. If I did not concentrate on foot placement my entire leg would just give way and I'd be in a heap on the ground in incredible pain. I remember hauling out bags of frozen food from the chest freezer in the garage and standing awkwardly. My knee gave way and I ended up in a heap on the ground. I was midway through a barbecue and party with dozens of people mingling in the late summer sun in our garden. I think this was the final straw for my now husband who spent the next two days trying to make inroads to the original consultant. My records had been misplaced! A few days later I was yet again inside an MRI tunnel. The results were rushed through, and the apologetic head of orthopaedic consulting was mumbling something about the curled up and completely detached ligament which was now miraculously visible (two years later) whereas clearly it was hidden behind the other ligament at the time of the injury. I translated this into please don't sue the hospital for this monumental cock-up. I was in surgery a week later for what I will always remember to be a much more painful procedure than childbirth. Recovery was excruciating, lengthy and painful. I had no choice other than survive and commit to the physiotherapy because in my wisdom I had booked myself onto a divemaster training course in Fort Lauderdale some four months later and I was not going to cancel it.

The repair included using the original ligament which with hindsight was a poor choice. It had shrivelled and curled up over the two years it had been disconnected so really it was never going to be in the best of shape. All the same it was re-stretched and screwed to the lower leg bone with an extra-long titanium screw. Because the ligament was now so tight the leg preferred to be straight, bending it was incredibly painful. Do I remember the pain? No, not the detail, but I did commit to memory the knowledge surgery on the ligaments will involve lengthy physiotherapy to retrain the ligament. Was I a more cautious skier post-surgery? Probably, but not consciously.

As with childbirth the pain of surgery is remembered only in the way we remember it was painful, we don't remember the actual pain. I can recall the detail of the event for the frustration with the French authorities and sniggering of the doctor at the resort. I can remember the phone calls from my insurance company who relayed the information that the snowboarder had been a French citizen and therefore his address, name and other details were being withheld from my English insurer. What better recommendation can a person have than to always use the insurer that was out of pocket to the tune of some five thousand pounds which couldn't be recovered due to French bureaucracy. When I say I remember the phone calls, I remember the general taste of the conversation, I don't remember the actual words. Everything else is a blur.

The middle of the road experiences are the most frequent. We don't remember them all and the ones we do remember commit only certain elements to long-term memory. I remember I had a broken collarbone, I have no recollection of how many golfers were in the minibus, I do remember all but the driver were women.

I remember being in a cubicle at a hospital with a man wearing white rubber gloves stitching up the side of my face, I cannot remember any other details. I remember the pain of falling off a rockface and landing on my feet and the shock that gave to my hips. I remember wondering what had happened to the climbing chock I had pushed into the crack on the rock face which should have protected me from such a fall. I remember taking a great deal of care in placing such security during future climbs and in some instances adding secondary protection. A bad experience led to extra caution. Did it stop me climbing? Of course not. Did it stop me from having other falls? No.

Middle of the road experiences are not all negative, many of them are positive. It's why I call them middle of road—they can veer in either direction, towards the negative or towards the positive. The problem is, the detail is sketchy. We take elements away from them and not necessarily in the right order, accuracy or in some cases, as they actually happened. We can embellish them to make them more than the sum of their real place in our memories. Often we remember nothing more than a colour, a location, a phrase, a taste or a person.

The details of our holidays will go into this category with a few exceptions of course. How many of your holidays can you truly remember in great detail? You may remember you had good experiences, or remember drinking too much at a beach party, or remember the one night you had to cook your own food using a pot of hot oil placed on your table, or the night you went skinny dipping. We seem to select elements of experiences and commit them to memory but they rarely reappear for use as an informative tool for choosing the next holiday, but rather as good after dinner conversation pieces. We should also remind ourselves how we remember events, activities and experiences is often not shared.

I conducted a small experiment on memory while I was working for Charles Sturt University in Goulburn, New South Wales. My

REAR-VIEW MIRROR

international Chinese students were all completing a joint policing degree and were part way through a module on statement taking from witnesses. Their instructions were to observe. I placed a large Mr Potato Head on the table alongside a mini version. The mini version was fully clothed while the larger version was naked. The students concentrated while I spent time adding eyes, facial features and clothing. I was deliberate in my actions confident they would remember the parts in great detail. It took me little more than five minutes at which point I threw a towel over the mini Mr Potato Head and asked them to work in pairs and reproduce it on sketch paper. The results were hilarious. Of course they had concentrated on my actions and not on the mini version alongside. I then played a small clip from *The Dark Knight* where the Joker is in the commercial kitchen slamming a villains head down on a pencil. They were asked to write down their full recollection of the scene using a standard police check sheet which included categories such as room description, people present, clothing, distinguishing features, time of day, weather and many more items. They worked in small groups then had to swap the sheets amongst the groups and re-watch the DVD clip marking each box for accuracy as we waded through the scene almost frame by frame. The inaccuracies were astounding but the learning almost immeasurable. Their homework was to take copies of *Vantage Point* home and watch it. The movie is a very clever observance on building a picture of an event from multiple individual vantage points without which the true facts would not be evident. The students had made copious notes. My only question was, what was the make of video camera Forest Whitaker was using to record the major events? Only one student had made such thorough notes they could answer the question. We all observe life from differing viewpoints. The learning objectives remained the same but instead of using a police worthy scenario and context, presenting it in an unexpected manner helped them better understand the complexity and difficulties.

My learning and experience from this was the students had seen neither movie before, as Western titles were banned in China. I then had to ponder whether I had broken any international laws allowing them to watch them as part of the course, but it didn't hang around as an issue in my mind for too long.

A lot of people may tell you they remember in great detail where they were and what they were doing for world stopping events such as JFK's assassination, or 9-11. Memories of these events have high dependency on involvement and location. A person standing on a grassy knoll is going to remember everything very differently to someone watching it unfold on television in a bar. There are thousands upon thousands of perspectives for 9-11.

It was a working day for me. I had just been promoted to principal lecturer in charge of a major project but I hadn't yet moved office. The university was still effectively in recess for the summer break so teaching staff were thin on the ground, but without anything better to do I was in my office, which would on a good day hold four lecturing staff. Today it was only me. I was working on some configuration issues for a recent version update to our virtual learning environment where the learning management system wasn't performing as well as it should, when a news ticker scrolled across the top of the screen. Yes 2001 was a very different computing world to today. *Attacks on World Trade Centre in New York* it ticked. I managed to load up the internet browser but the page refused to refresh. At this point the entire system seemed to freeze and I was unable to do anything with the screen. I rebooted it but it resulted in the same dumb logic. I left my office and checked other offices. There were only one or two other lecturing staff in the building so I made my way up the four flights of stairs to the Head of School's office where little was going on there either. A few more shrugged shoulders from the catering staff in the coffee bar and I decided enough was enough. On with the motorbike clothing and off home to find my son stood in front of the television screen. It was forty-five minutes after Flight 11 was deliberately flown into the North Tower. Thirty minutes later the South Tower collapsed followed another thirty minutes later by the North Tower. I have no idea what we did for food on that day, whether my son went to college or his part-time work in the evening. I do remember watching rolling television coverage switching from news channel to news channel to see if they were broadcasting anything different. This would be a day etched in millions of people's memories, each of us with a different viewpoint. Some were there inside the towers, responding as part of the emergency services or on New York's streets, while many others around the globe were watching on TV or listening to the events unfold on the radio. We would perhaps automatically run through what-if scenarios. My university had staff in New York on the day. What if, what if. I have this in my middle of the road category whereas other people will most certainly have it in road crash. For those of us not directly affected thankfully it doesn't rise from our long-term memory too often. For those involved or affected by it, this day will never be forgotten.

Ultimate road trips

The birth of a first child fits easily into this category. As women we may remember in fine detail a lot from our experience of childbirth. The smells, the room, the attending staff, the repair surgery (yuck), the first tentative look at the baby, the instant love, the tears, the doting grandparents, the tearful partner, the tiredness, the flowers. I was alone in the delivery room for the birth of my son, except of course for the wonderful and attentive staff. My husband could not bear to see 'any of that'! No wonder I divorced him. Do you have the same level of detail for the memories of subsequent births?

Flying to Buenos Aires and transferring to Ushuaia to sit astride a BMW700GS to ride to Pucon. Ushuaia, the Straits of Magellan, the wind, Torres del Paine and the eco-camp, the barbecue on bricks and the freezing cold night, the guanaco crossing the road, the condors circling above Mt Fitzroy at El Chaltén, ice carving off the Perito Merino glacier, the metal stickman sculpture at El Calafate, the ski lodges at Bariloche, the smoking volcano, the crystal clear spring waters and waterfalls, the stunning scenery and finally Pucon. This would be the romantic memories. What about the roller-coaster ride out on a trip boat from Ushuaia into some of the roughest waters in the world to look at seals and birdlife. Or the snow that hit us riding the bikes on day one as we climbed up over the mountain out of Ushuaia. The local maps and wall paintings depicting the Falkland Islands as the Malvinas and whatever you do don't mention your British heritage. The endless gravel roads and the constant incredibly strong winds. Riverbed crossings and wet feet. Mud and sand instead of roads. The endurance necessary to ride for hundreds of kilometres each day. More incredible scenery. It was an amazing journey. Mind-numbing at times and the concentration required on what was effectively 85% off-road riding on super rough terrain would clear away thoughts of any kind. For that reason it was a rejuvenating, come back new type of journey. The kind of journey that doesn't fill a hole in the psyche it creates a lust for another one. So much so in fact we did it again a few years later this time from Iquique in Chile to Machu Picchu in Peru. Yet again the memories of the cities and towns were indelible but I remember this amazing journey with some negative caveats. My left knee was clearly weakened at this point. It was six years since the ligament repair and something was wrong. The knee didn't have strength and I could tell from my own apprehension I was not keen on taxing the leg too much. At the end of each gruelling day the pain in the knee was mind-numbing. Eventually the lack of confidence in my leg's ability to hold up the bike should I encounter challenging enough terrain, resulted in me hitting a rock and the bike going over. I tried to save the bike but my left foot stamped at the rough ground which sent a huge jerk right up my left leg. For a minute or more I believed my left knee repair had snapped as the pain was so intense. Then almost as soon as it started the pain subsided. I could hardly believe it. The incident affected my riding confidence for the rest of the journey.

My other lasting memory of this incredible adventure was the result of the altitude sickness medication we were taking. It affected my husband in ways no-one could have predicted. It was at the hotel in Potosi, home to one of the world's oldest and almost entirely exhausted silver mines in Bolivia, we would discover varicose veins don't always affect only the legs. My husband emerged from the shower that morning with blood running down his legs. On close examination, as one does to a loved one, I could see he had ruptured varicose veins on his scrotum. Among our group were a couple from Victoria who would become dear friends. She offered some ladies sanitary pads which brought great laughter from the rest of the group who were nearly all men. A quick call was made to the local doctor who advised immediately ceasing his blood pressure medication and the altitude sickness medication. After an hour everything had dried up but he still wore the pads as a comfort layer much to the continued amusement of his fellow male riders.

My lasting negative memory of the trip is of La Paz, where I spent a whole day in bed in between bouts of being violently ill having descended rapidly into the bowl that surrounds the city. It seems altitude sickness is not just about ascending, but also the result of descending too quickly.

My lasting positive memory was of the incredible ride into Ollantaytambo train station over narrow cobbled streets with hairpin switchbacks. From there we boarded what must be one of the most scenic trains in the world which would take us to Aguas Calientes at the foot of Machu Picchu where we spent the night. We ate at a restaurant where guinea pig on a stick was the delicacy. Next morning, we had to be up at five to catch the coach up the mountain to the ruins. I remember the ridiculous narrowness of the road only wide enough for a single bus, which brought huge intakes of breath when a descending bus would present in front of us wanting to pass. In my mind I would make a mental note to google how many buses had ended up toppling off the road down the unimaginably steep mountain sides, resulting in the death of everyone onboard.

Apart from the birth of my son, and possibly the collection from the dealer of my first motorbike, my ultimate road trips are literal. Travel along with scuba diving combine to make one big passion and form the bulk of my positive memories. Even when working oversees I would always find time to head out and explore. My memory can easily recall the golden statue at the Rockefeller Centre, the base of the Statue of Liberty, the helicopter ride over the Grand Canyon, taking the weirdly configured lift up to the room in the Luxor Hotel in Las Vegas, the art deco bar on the permanently decommissioned Queen Mary at Long Beach, watching space shuttle *Columbia* lift off from the other side of the Banana River, being hauled back inside the cage off Port Lincoln when a great white cruised past in front, lying on top of the Betty Bomber at the bottom of Truk Lagoon, my first shark feed on the Great Barrier Reef, the cod hole, my first Blue Jays game in Toronto, the first time I stood on the glass floor of the CN Tower, watching the Fridge play for the Chicago Bears, the steam clock in Vancouver, the Olympic stadium in Montreal, Niagara, the elephants at Tsavo West, diving with crocodile fish off Mombasa, seeing Kilimanjaro from the air, the endless border crossings in South America, the colourful dress of the ladies of the floating Uros Islands of Lake Titicaca, Eileen Donan castle and the hot chocolate in the café, Thunder Road restaurant in Dublin where my husband proposed, my son taking his one and only scuba dive in Sea World Edinburgh, seeing my son being presented with his BA in Journalism in Lincoln, my first static line parachute jump, my 90th skydive, my first bungee jump off a crane and my second one in Cairns QLD, jumping off the Auckland tower in New Zealand, feeding a giraffe at Taronga Zoo, Alcatraz, Hoover Dam, crossing the Golden Gate bridge, Monument Valley, watching New Year fireworks at the twin towers in Kuala Lumpur, Death Valley, the helicopter flight up to Taku Glacier in Alaska, Honiara, Philip Island race circuit, seeing my husband fly a Tiger Moth at Duxford in the UK, Hamilton Island, the War Memorial in Canberra, the Blue Room Sydney Harbour for New Year's Eve (twice), swimming with dolphins Kimbit and Spunky at Key Largo, seeing the car in which JFK was shot at the Ford Museum in Detroit, bribing customs officers with whisky just to get into Lagos in Nigeria for work, Disneyland Florida, riding off-road bikes in Cyprus, having too much lead weight on my initial wreck dive on the Zenobia, flying in a light aircraft over Uluru and Kata Tjuta, descending into the Jenolan Caves, climbing as a fourteen-year-old alongside Chris Bonnington in Borrowdale, being in the same room as Sir David Attenborough (along with about three thousand other people), and absolutely countless other incredible adventures.

It is the ultimate road trips which lift us up. We might remember them for the adrenalin or the euphoria, or the sense of achievement, or being in the presence of a great human being, or an astonishing animal or bird but we do remember them. An extraordinary experience may never be repeated, perhaps that's why we capture them in such detail. We experience, we learn, we remember, we recall. In my life I seek them out. It is these elements of our lives which bring balance, renewal, enlightenment, revelation. These **EVOLUTIONARY MOMENTS** are the ones that **ACTIVATE GROWTH**. Experiencing them has exposed me to unbelievable journeys, different cultures, my own limitations, enjoyment, happiness, emersion, activities, nature and much more. Each ultimate road trip results in the evolution of the personality, knowledge and wisdom. Your evolutionary moments might be a completely different shape. Trekking, marathon running, fast car racing, ballroom dancing competition, acting in a play, building an engine, playing championship golf or cooking dinner for one hundred homeless people. The common theme is personal growth. You are a better, more fulfilled person as a result of these moments.

Spending too much time looking in the **REAR-VIEW MIRROR**, stuck inside our own minds ruminating and dwelling on past events, experiences and memories is where we get stuck. While it is good to revisit positive memories, often we find the more negative memories are both debilitating and tiring.

YOUR LAST SELF-HELP BOOK

In trying to understand how the mind stores and recalls memories now is a good time to take a look in the **REAR-VIEW MIRROR.**

- Make a list of your definitive **ROAD CRASH EXPERIENCES**
- Do the same for your **MIDDLE OF THE ROAD EXPERIENCES**
- List your **ULTIMATE ROAD TRIPS**

Concentrating on your **ROAD CRASH EXPERIENCE** list, expand on each one in as much detail as you are comfortable writing down. Try to use bullet points although sentences are also fine.

ROUNDABOUTS

YOUR LAST SELF-HELP BOOK

'You learn something new every day if you pay attention.'
                                              Ray LeBlond

'I don't think much of a man who is not wiser today than he was yesterday.'
                                              Abraham Lincoln

It is here that we can be stuck. We circle around, unable to make a decision about where to go next. Not being able to leave the relative safety of the roundabout even though it is boring as batshit circling around and around, is where we create ruts and furrows in our journey. Your roundabouts may present themselves after a **ROAD CRASH EXPERIENCE**, or as a result of something else. The roundabout is overflowing with our patterns and habits. Here, we dwell on the past, we get far too comfortable in the present, and we feel unable to visualise the future. Often we spend far too much time imagining fanciful scenarios, and impossible futures. Identifying what is keeping us circling the roundabout is how we can recognise the patterns or habit, and break free of its chains.

The Past has an annoying habit of resurrecting itself when we don't want it to. But, it can also be useful. We hated that hotel by the beach, we're not going to go back there but we liked the town so we'll hunt out somewhere else closer to our favourite restaurant and pub. We really like the look of those training shoes but the heel is too low and may result in blisters so we'll try some from the competition instead. Past experience helps shape our future choices. Except now, we have been offered a new job which requires office wear. Can I get away with wearing those training shoes but in black instead of formal dress shoes? Probably not. We now enter a new memory game, the type where we create scenarios and scenes in order to arrive at a solution or solve something that's puzzling us.

ROUNDABOUTS

Our lives are the sum total of the choices we have made. Repeating patterns are human nature—we like habits. For some of us, those habits are not necessarily positive. While living with my mother, my weekly Saturday duties involved dusting and collecting lunch from the fish and chip shop. Dusting had to be conducted in a certain way and in a certain order. Was my mother extremely tidy or did it go further than that? She had a wooden cigar box. Turned sideways this had to be used to align the thousand or so books with the front edge of the shelf. Once a month all of the books had to be taken off the shelf so dust could be removed from behind them. Replacing the books involved banging them together to make sure the top of each book had no dust. They were all replaced in the right order and lined up using the cigar box. Ornaments had to be dusted and replaced in exactly the same location facing the *right* way. The same with the vinyl collection, the chair cushions, the magazines in the rack, the bathroom accessories on the window sill, the plants in the kitchen, the music in the piano stool. They were not my habits but I had to learn a process. The repetition, learning the actions in order to complete the process, were a transferred habit. The long-term effect has been that cleaning my own home is not a simple process. I have built my own habits based on this learning. My mother clearly had some degree of obsessive-compulsive disorder. Have I inherited OCD or I am just repeating a learned habit and process? It's an interesting question isn't it? I am the sum product of my upbringing.

Few people would rarely consider having a permanently tidy house an issue, the wider problem is when keeping it tidy impacts others. In my case it is my husband that has to follow the rules I impose for positioning our items and artefacts. Over the years the anxiety of not having items dust free or tidily hanging in the wardrobe has lessened, but I still get anxious when change is necessary such as having to endure the dust from sanding something ready for painting, or having to move furniture in order to clean underneath. Would it keep me circling the roundabout if the house were a mess? Yes, I believe it would.

Many other habits keep us circling the roundabout. Some are driven out of necessity such as taking the kids to the same school to arrive at the same time, or taking them to sporting events in which they are actively engaged. Or commuting to work, or stopping at the same coffee shop on the way in or out on the journey to work. Our lives do seem to revolve around some big universal habits. Work hours, school hours, five-day weeks, two-day weekends, two weeks on holiday, two sugars in a cup of tea, certain brands of bread, favourite pubs and restaurants always at the same time on set days. The animal kingdom is filled with creatures of habit.

Our habits can influence the direction we take, or don't take. Our chosen career, even our employer can all bind us to the feeling of circling the roundabout. Not everyone wants to escape it, but some really do want a change—but either don't have enough faith in themselves to exit, or don't know which exit to take.

I worked for the UK government for ten years, with a short intervention to give birth to my son, and was really in a negative slump. While I had been well-trained in project management, the role itself had slow progression and was realistically dead men's shoes. My department was information technology but I wanted to do more, be more, progress more, so I decided to exit in favour of a new road and applied for and was accepted into university. I had to enter at diploma level as I had been out of education for so long. It was effectively the foundation, transferring into undergraduate Bachelor of Science and then on to Master of Science degrees. I loved it. An **EVOLUTIONARY MOMENT** where I not only recognised my own abilities, but could clearly see a whole network of roads opening up off the roundabout. A definitive **ACTIVATED GROWTH** moment.

More often people stick with the roundabout out of fear of the unknown, a lack of self-belief, or inability to picture a new direction. We are also influenced by bad experiences and the memories they leave behind. Changing careers is not only daunting it takes courage

ROUNDABOUTS

to leave the relative safety of one job for another. Even when writing a resume or application letter the mind is milling and drilling through memories of work experiences, colleagues, managers, environment and more. Positives and negatives will be drawn out of the long-term memory which can affect whether an application is submitted or not. Staying put is often the lesser of the evils. Once the idea of change is withdrawn the potential candidate can return to circling the roundabout. So the pattern continues.

We are kept circling the roundabout by our limiting beliefs. For whatever reason we have reached an impasse in our minds. Our experiences, memories, ideas and convictions are preventing us from moving forward. For some, this is not a bad thing. For others, we are being controlled by fake limitations and fences which are the creation of nothing more than the mind. We must find a way to move beyond the limiting belief and knock down the controlling fence.

The Present is where we should place ourselves for most of the time, if only it were that easy. This is where our everyday tasks exist. We may plan (future self) in advance, or we may look backward (past self) to arrive at this point, but ultimately we need to live in the moment. The 'moment' is our general existence. It is filled with our routine habitual tasks such as picking up the kids, shopping on a Monday, attending the gym, getting animal fodder, in fact a huge number of things we do almost without pre-planning or prior thought. These tasks should not need intellectual analysis or deep thinking beyond perhaps passing a driving test, applying for a credit card, opening a bank account or completing the many sets of forms we'll come across during the course of our lives. These are activities we complete time and again, almost habitually, on automatic. We don't need to think much about filling the dishwasher or filling the kitchen sink to handwash dishes. Some of this is learned experience and is done via recall from memory. New thinking is only necessary when something different needs washing, such as delicate china or an oddly shaped item. There may be a brief journey into long-term memory for the last time you washed something similar, but rarely are new strains of thought created. It is here however in the present, that new learning takes place. Whether that be by coursework or formal or informal teaching, a brand-new never tried before activity, a holiday to a new town or country, the first journey on a boat, the first attendance at an event or seeing a band for the first time, they all contribute to our experience and pass into memory. The more we expose ourselves to new activities and new learning, the broader our knowledge becomes, and the more we have in our memories to draw upon.

When we engage in experiential learning or by engagement in teaching, we process the knowledge and information from the activity and record it in memory. We are richer today than we were yesterday as a result.

The Future is where we have never been and in theory, can never get because it will always be the future. We can attempt to predict it but in reality it unfolds before our eyes. Our problem here is the scenarios we visualise in order to try and materialise our preferred future or in some cases, to ensure it doesn't materialise.

We often try to visualise what will happen. We've received an email from the HR Manager and we've been called to a meeting the following morning. No other information is provided. Are we going to be given our marching orders, given a promotion, reprimanded or given a warning, or asked to mentor a new employee? All of these possible scenarios are running through our mind. More often than not we'll settle on the worst-case scenario. We've decided we've done something wrong and therefore we're going to be given a written warning, or worse we're going to be given our notice and asked to leave. In amongst all of that are toe-curling scenes involving thumping of tables, drama school performances, coffee cups, free sandwiches, the time we were given a written warning for writing on the school walls and a dozen other imaginary, real or unrealistic scenes. In the end we've wasted hours trying to predict the future. Now, had we been rehearsing what we may say at a job interview, that

ROUNDABOUTS

would be worthwhile, but deleting a few hours of life and building stress over maybes, is a roundabout moment. We are stuck on it, circling round and around trying to solve a puzzle which has yet to be constructed. This is something that we do far too often. It's a pattern of behaviour that we fall into, and a habit which is not easy to break.

The likely, the possible and the downright improbable—aka—the fanciful

If you have done something at work that is really beyond your job description, talked to someone inappropriately, then it's **likely** that the meeting with HR will be about that incident. If the conversation while inappropriate was to advise someone their actions were dangerous, unnecessary or uncalled for and you took the lead in preventing some form of accident the conversation to reward you for your quick actions is **possible**. If you didn't realise that the person you were talking to was the richest man in Queensland, and while he didn't take too kindly to being spoken to in that manner, he has still talked to the manager and conveyed his wish to buy you a superyacht as a reward, well that's going to be **downright improbable**. The likelihood of a scenario maturing however, didn't stop you from running through all three of them in your mind, in the space of a few minutes. It is also probable that the scenario which has the greatest personal impact, will be the one which you dwell on the longest, expending the most negative energy and giving you the greatest angst and stress often to the degree you would consider calling in sick so you don't have to face the music. You will note after the event (having been told that the employee you spoke to has been dismissed for failing to provide the appropriate police check documentation, and the reason you are in the office is to discuss covering her shifts for the next two weeks) what a monumental waste of time and effort the previous evening's mind mining had been. Even having made the mental note, it won't deter or stop you from expending the same amount of energy on the next unexplained event.

YOUR LAST SELF-HELP BOOK

This is how we churn through possibility. Of course there are thousands of examples. Someone leaves a short message on the phone to return a call. You haven't heard from them in months and last time they called it was to tell you their elderly parent, your Aunt was ill. You instantly run to the knowledge you do have which is the illness, coupled with the person's age and previous history. Before you know it you're already planning what you're going to wear to the funeral. When you do manage to return the call, you are asked if you know anyone who does engine repairs on the cheap as a good friend of theirs who lives near to you has overheated their car!

The time that we spend inside our own heads can be positive but also destructive. We can purposefully rehearse what we will say at a job interview. We can try to predict the questions which will be asked and compile suitable answers. We make mental notes to do things, we remember we need something which is not on the shopping list, we remember the car needs fuel and we run through our memory for the nearest suitable fuel stop. We like a certain fuel station because they always have good coffee. We like shopping at the same supermarket because we've already done the due diligence aisle by aisle which means we can be in and out in no time without having to hunt too much for the items we need. These kinds of thoughts are transient and usually positive. This is not, however, where our mind wants to dwell; it would rather sink its teeth into negativity, worrying about things which may never happen, but thinking about them anyway. The question may be, how do we stop circling the roundabout and exit onto a more productive road?

ROUNDABOUTS

Think about your roundabout moments. These are the points in our lives where we get stuck. Unable to let go of the job we hate. Unable to let go of the relationship which isn't working. Unable to move past a grievance or something negative in the workplace. Perhaps there is a person(s) who inflicts emotional or physical trauma which pins you to thinking and rethinking about the trauma or the person.

Pinpoint at least two instances for each of the categories.

- The past
- The present
- The future
- The fanciful

If necessary, give each of these instances a nickname, or a category so they can be more easily recalled and referred to. You may come up with less or more, everyone is different.

ROADBLOCKS

YOUR LAST SELF-HELP BOOK

'Repetition of the same thought or physical action develops into a habit which, repeated frequently enough, becomes an automatic reflex.'

Norman Vincent Peale

'Moral excellence comes about as a result of habit. We become just by doing just acts, temperate by doing temperate acts, brave by doing brave acts.'

Aristotle

Roadblocks include our hang-ups. A psychological or emotional block. A fixation or a preoccupation. They are limiting in their repetition, and in their ability to prevent us from moving forward. Perfectionism, toxic people, people who claim they are always right and you are wrong, anger, jealousy, shame, pain, distrust, resentment, self-imposed commitment to family/ social groups/ organisations, not letting go of past events and your own ego to name but a few common hang-ups.

Experiencing assault reintroduced roadblocks I had long ago consigned to long-term memory. My learning point here is that nothing is truly forgotten or eradicated, it is only parked. It also introduced something new, disbelief. The assault reintroduced resentment, anger, questioning, reduced self-belief, anguish, anxiety, fear and shame, none of which produce positive energy, only negative feelings and emotions. But disbelief this could happen to me at all, was something new.

My feelings while centring on the assailant spread to other people who had been in the room at the time. They also spread to those who would pass comment and judgement, but who were not present. I

ROADBLOCKS

am still dumbfounded by those who would post an opinion based on second-hand information and rumour, often omitting or altering facts to garner support for their preferred side. Those people were not in the room on the day so any information they have is second-hand and potentially skewed in favour of one side or the other. It never ceases to amaze me how facts morph into fiction after only a few days. It used to be referred to as Chinese whispers. My imaginary scales were weighed down by disbelief that one person was now asking for thoughts to be sent out to the accused in case he 'did something silly'! People who did not know me but who clearly knew the accused were offering him support. People who had instantly supported me flipped for no apparent reason to support him. All of these actions produced in me resentment and anger. Having to negotiate my own emotions as a result, was unwelcome and an abomination to me. How dare people support the accused. How dare people question the truth of the matter. How dare people try to play down the ferocity of the event.

As time passes we begin to second guess our actions. We question and challenge what we know to be true as doubt sets in. His belligerence created anguish and anxiety, and the lack of even the most meagre apology to his peers or to me, made me question the incident even more. Had I taken the right action reporting this to the police? Should I have gone further given this was a workplace? Why had I not said anything in retaliation to him at the time? Should I have physically retaliated? Why was I not worthy of my role in the organisation? Why was he allowed to return to work? Why was he allowed to share the same office space? Why was he allowed to continue as if nothing had happened? Why was he allowed to cause emotional trauma? All of these emotions, thoughts and feelings were roadblocks. I was unable to move beyond them for months. Every time he entered a room I felt anguish and anxiety, once to the point of uncontrolled tears. I had created a bubble of resilience based on mutual respect. I had unbounded respect for everyone I came into contact with, even those with opposing views had they taken the time to get to know me better and understand my personality. Discovering this level of respect was not reflected back at me made me pause and think. At one point I was driven to seek documentary evidence in the form of statutory declarations where one person had consistently tried to defame me, and knock down my reputation. Then I found myself seeking out and gathering more of them. As though having small pieces of paper from closely aligned allies brought some form of comfort. They didn't, not really. There were people out there in the community who voiced the opposing view of 'she deserved it'. This view I refused to reconcile. I had no slot in which to park this information, the accusations, or the assault. The event kept rolling around in my mind. I had partially lost my resilience, my ability to bounce back and recover. I was back in the bedroom with the tiger prowling on the landing.

Our roadblocks stop us from moving forward. When we come across a roadblock sometimes the effects are so debilitating we can't even perform everyday tasks. We shrink into the security of our favourite locations. Perhaps the bedroom, perhaps the couch. When my partner John died, I had crashed into the roadblock head-on. In my experience the roadblock is a permanent feature. It is not something which can be removed, which can be crushed, which can be driven over. The roadblock resembles an insurmountable concrete monolith. The road on the other side, the road we were travelling down, is no longer accessible to us. We are stuck behind the concrete until we can find a way around it, having created a brand-new route. Roadblocks **ACTIVATE CHANGE**, not always immediately, but eventually. We either have to backtrack to the last junction or go off-road.

Backtracking for me is a refusal to deal with the issue. We have decided to **ACTIVATE CHANGE** but instead of finding a new path we park the issue. This doesn't bring resolution but instead allows the issue to fester and suppurate. It lies dormant and rears its ugly head all too often.

It was 2013 when I dropped the motorbike en-route to Machu Picchu thinking I had ripped the repaired ligament out from the titanium screw that was holding it in place. It would take another three years for the meniscus, the padding between the thigh bone and the lower leg bone behind the knee cap to break down sufficiently to warrant another MRI scan. Three years before I acted on the knowledge that the knee was further damaged. Three years of intermittent pain. Three years of procrastination.

Surgery was needed in September 2016 to remove half of the meniscus so the leg would bend, to confirm that the screw was still in place, but also to reveal that the repaired ligament had stretched to well beyond useful. Here I was, yet again in the hands of the physiotherapist, with a set and laborious routine, working to regain full extension of the knee. Only this time the surgery came with a warning, there would be no skiing, and motorbiking would be limited due to the danger of a fall which could fully dislodge the ligament. Well I don't know about you, but if someone says, 'you can't, you shouldn't, or don't do something', it almost skips over the top of my knowledge bank and falls right out of the back of my head. It's a red flag. The silk waved in the bullring. Can't, shouldn't and don't is translated in my mind to find a way to bypass those words. My next question would be, what about a knee brace? It was not met with wholehearted positivity but I took the contorted face as a maybe. That was all I needed. I hunted down the most effective extreme carbon skeleton knee brace I could find designed for extreme athletes, which was fitted in Adelaide but manufactured and moulded in the United States. The day it arrived, I booked a two week off and on-road tour of Rajasthan on a Royal Enfield. I had paid thousands of dollars for a world-class knee brace and didn't need to try it out to convince myself it would support my leg. My research told me everything I needed to know. This is confidence in action. Spending over two weeks in India wearing it on some fairly degraded roads proved the point.

I knew I had to **ACTIVATE CHANGE** but instead of seeking out a solution on return to Australia in 2013, I backtracked to acceptance that the knee was damaged and I would endure the occasional session of pain. Had I listened to my own theories and to my own body, I would have gone off-road immediately and the result would probably have been the whole meniscus would still be intact, and offering better padding for many more years to come. Instead, I am probably much closer to a full knee replacement, which cannot be something anyone should look forward to. I don't have to dig too far for a reason for the delay, the knowledge the original repair surgery had been incredibly painful. Revisiting that pain and the sheer hard work of physiotherapy kept reaching out from its parked slot in the mind. Sometimes our ability to reason and formulate our own best solution floats just underneath the surface, yet we refuse to act on it. Had I set the goal of riding in India earlier, perhaps the motivation to purchase the brace would have come sooner.

There are no wrong decisions. We are presented with choices and we apply environmental and other influencing factors to those choices to arrive at a decision. Investigate knee surgery now, or wait. I have learnt over time a decision well founded is quickly assigned its permanent parking slot. A decision made on the run, or lacking enough due diligence to meet an individual's criteria for sound reflection and process, is not immediately parked. This leaves a gap for compassionate and empathetic (and negative and self-serving) people to try and influence the decision. They may not be privy to every factor being applied to the decision point. But the point of the intervention is the moment doubt can creep in, and we start second-guessing our own choices. Life is a lengthy learning journey. Going off-road may mean using stepping stones to move around the roadblock. There may be innumerable stones to choose from, or only one or two. Having chosen the next stone, stick with it and step forward. Do not be tempted onto a different stone by other people. Choose the next step carefully, and stick with it.

Going off-road is seeking help. We have deviated from the route and need some form of assistance. It may come in many forms. Counselling, support groups, peer groups, education, training, retraining, mentoring, family, friends, medical interventions, mental health interventions, respite, relocation, even legal assistance.

ROADBLOCKS

There is no shame in seeking assistance. Taking on someone else's perspective, can add clarity and build resilience and either confirm your position or supersede it, or ultimately, be discarded. The decision is now informed. It can be confined, it's a package, it's not the best you can come up with it is the 'right' decision now, step forward and don't look back.

It should also be noted a roadblock can be self-imposed for good, and bad reasons. On our recent Royal Enfield tour of Rajasthan, we detoured off-road down steep terrain to have lunch at an eco-camp positioned on the edge of a vast lake, surrounded by incredible bird and wildlife. Going down was not so hard as the descent was controlled by the brakes. The terrain was sheets of smoothed and weathered layered rock with the occasional fissure or challenging switch back. The route we had to take was precise and loaded with hazards. After lunch everyone jumped on the bikes for the return ride. Wisdom, age and common sense all came to the party, superseding my self-belief and ego. I asked one of the support drivers to ride the bike up the cliff. He grinned. Our tour group were all very competent riders so up to this point he had no opportunity to ride one of the bikes. I travelled in the jeep following the group up the steep climb. Ascending steep and difficult terrain requires throttle control and an ability to ride slowly. The throttle has to be opened to edge over any minor obstruction, but closing it off too quickly can cause the bike to judder or stall which often results in a loss of balance and the bike being dropped. There were a few *foot down* moments and one minor topple but nothing serious. At the top I faced some questioning looks. 'I know my limitations,' I stated. I know my ability and I'm very capable of riding even the toughest terrain however, I'm not wearing a two-thousand-dollar carbon knee brace for no reason and I'm not keen on a knee replacement on the wrong side of sixty years of age.

Take experience and knowledge, and apply good judgement and we have wisdom. Trying to predict the future, while revisiting time and again the past just causes anxiety and unnecessary stress. Had I known the evening before we were *expected* to ride over sheet rock up a steep climb I know where my mind would have been. I know because my mind has been there before in South America. Riding incredibly difficult terrain in Patagonia for close to three weeks, certainly brought some degree of anxiety to each day, especially near the end of the tour when we were all tired and aching. I completed that adventure riding the bike every day for the whole three-thousand kilometres although it must be said, my leg was not quite as damaged at the time. Having the experience parked in my long-term memory however, meant the prior learning tried to create barriers. So, not knowing about the sheet rock in India meant I could go straight to bypassing the experience, instead of worrying about it for the days prior. We don't have to be heroes, we don't have anything to prove. We just need the decision to be authentic and honest.

We all have roadblocks and they mostly sit inside our psychology and emotions. They can be fixations or preoccupation, and are generally classified as hang-ups. I gave the following examples at the beginning of this chapter—perfectionism, toxic people, people who claim they are always right and you are wrong, anger, jealousy, shame, pain, distrust, resentment, self-imposed commitment to family/ social groups/ organisations, not letting go of past events and your own ego. This is a tiny snapshot, there are many more. It is something we seem incapable of knocking out of the way or jumping over. We have to bypass them.

> List five to ten roadblocks, the things you can't remove from your personality, the emotional barriers which prevent progression.

STALLED

YOUR LAST SELF-HELP BOOK

'If you always put a limit on everything you do, physical or anything else, it will spread into your work and into your life. There are no limits. There are only plateaus, and you must not stay there, you must go beyond them.'

Bruce Lee

'Procrastination is the bad habit of putting off until the day after tomorrow what should have been done the day before yesterday.'

Napoleon Hill

The roundabout is indecision, the rut, a pattern, safety and comfort. The roadblock, is a sudden stop. It requires you to **ACTIVATE CHANGE**, or **ACTIVATE GROWTH** in order to get past it. The roadblock may morph into an **EVOLUTIONARY MOMENT**. When you are stalled, you can see the light at the end of the tunnel but have neither the motivation, means nor energy to move towards it.

Our twenty acres hosts a variety of farm animals and birds. We purchased the land in 2014. It was previously a Geraldton waxflower farm and was littered with knocked over bushes, tyres and green plastic tree protector bags. With the grant of planning we built the house and huge shed and started to repurpose a lot of the old irrigation poles to create animal shelters. We'd become good friends with the builders, so after numerous trips to their construction yards we had corrugated iron, more wood, roofing materials and all manner of offcuts of building waste products. From these recycled products we built fences, goat shelters, sheep sheds, a chook run and a duck enclosure. It's hard work, building the unfamiliar with little to no experience, but it is rewarding—and apart from screws and nails, all of it was free.

STALLED

After two years of constant construction and building we began to stall. Looking for excuses to not have to go out and work in the paddocks is a certain sign of reduced motivation. Working the land can be labour intensive and repetitive just as many industrial, manufacturing, farming and agricultural roles are. It's not easy, in fact in some cases it's impossible to introduce excitement or reward. Born into farming and the farming life means being born into the routine and way of life for a particular location and farm. Coming to it in later years as we were, is missing some vital elements such as parental or grandparents influence and knowledge, living the elders' way of life, and the learning they bring through the growing years. It's not to say it can't be done—it can—but it's a different journey and potentially a more solitary one without the element of early learning. An enquiring or searching mind needs stimulation, and the thought of repairing fencing or staining animal shelters, was not feeding that need. This is where diversification comes to the table. This is where innovation seeps in. Plant something new or unusual? Farm an unusual animal perhaps for wool or meat? Can enough vegetables be grown to supply a small market stall?

When we arrived in South Australia in 2013 we made a conscious decision to track down a location which had un-serviced land. No power, no direct water supply, no mains sewerage or any other utilities. Our power system is solar and batteries. We harvest all of our own rainwater and we have a soakage trench septic system to capture all of our sewerage. We produce very little garbage as we compost food waste and much of our paper waste. We use reverse-cycle air conditioners for heating and cooling so we don't require wood for burning. Our system has a backup generator which keeps us connected to fuel usage and our hot water, cooktop and oven run off gas, so we're still connected (albeit via bottles) to the gas grid.

Farmers might diversify with different animals, grow different crops, process some of their own produce, mix farming, offer accommodation or farm experiences. With our home only sitting on twenty acres we were limited to the number of animals each paddock would take.

We were keen on producing wool but not on meat sheep. Fruit, nut and olive trees have gone into the orchard we've developed, but we wanted to concentrate on growing only enough vegetables for our own consumption, and perhaps to use for bartering. We keep bees and produce raw honey. Apart from traditional employment, twenty acres of open canvas on the face of it, does not offer much by way of potential income. We could increase the number of beehives. We could plant an unusual high-value crop. We could start welding artistic garden ornaments. Some if not all of those activities would involve a steep learning curve. We had been city dwellers with little previous contact with the land other than enjoying it for leisure purposes. As a lateral thinker it didn't take long for me to arrive at my **EVOLUTIONARY MOMENT.** With a background in designing learning solutions it was obvious: author a short course on off-grid living. My experience and skills were used to evolve and grow our financial position. Couple this with my dual background in information technology and online learning solutions, and there was also an opening for marketing opportunities using social media. The stall morphed into motion, the motion brought new motivation and energy. I was on the move again.

> *'Most people don't have that willingness to break bad habits. They have a lot of excuses and they talk like victims.'*
> **Carlos Santana**

The stalled zone is filled with excuses. We're not good enough, we can't do that, I can't write today because the (insert excuse) needs cleaning, the (insert excuse) needs making, I can't find the (insert excuse), I need to go to (insert excuse) before I do anything, the (insert excuse) needs servicing, my clothes aren't (insert excuse) and a thousand other reasons for keeping your feet firmly stuck in the mud. Our favourite excuses include work, family, kids, money, home, time. Wake up. There is no wall you can't climb over, knock over or detour around.

STALLED

When we are stalled, we find it easy to sit on the roundabout. It was easy to stay in a UK government job for ten years because of the compensation. Guaranteed pension, guaranteed role (well almost), annual leave increasing with every additional year above eight years (not now), guaranteed pay rises (it was the 80s), plus the extras such as a library next door, subsidised technology, and when it came in a free mobile phone. It's easy to see how stability and security overpower risk and excitement.

Boredom and stagnation were driving me downwards. I was at a stop. My mind was dwelling on the past and the what-ifs. There was no light at the end of this tunnel only sadness, zero motivation and a deep sense of worthlessness. A few of my skydiving friends were talking about university. Some years of financial pain but for long-term gain. The more our small group talked, the more I realised there was possibility. The longer I left the application forms on the table, the further away the idea floated. When I was sitting in a group of like-minded people talking the idea up, everything was possible (through beer goggles of course). But when I was on my own, all of the gremlins of doubt crept in. So, how do we get past being stalled? Sometimes it comes down to simplicity. We stay in the rut feeling miserable, or we climb out of it. That far back in my life I know I would have sat down and examined the pros and cons. I would have weighed up both and automatically come up with more cons than pros—and why? Because that's what we prefer to do. If we have decided to make a decision based on indecision we'll load the bases in the negative rather than take a leap toward the positive.

YOUR LAST SELF-HELP BOOK

First recognise your limitations. Small steps and small decisions which move you forward are better than none at all.

- Is there light at the end of the tunnel?
- Where do you want to go?
- What do you ultimately want out of life?
- What motivates you?
- What is stopping you from moving forward?
- Are your stopping points real or perceived?

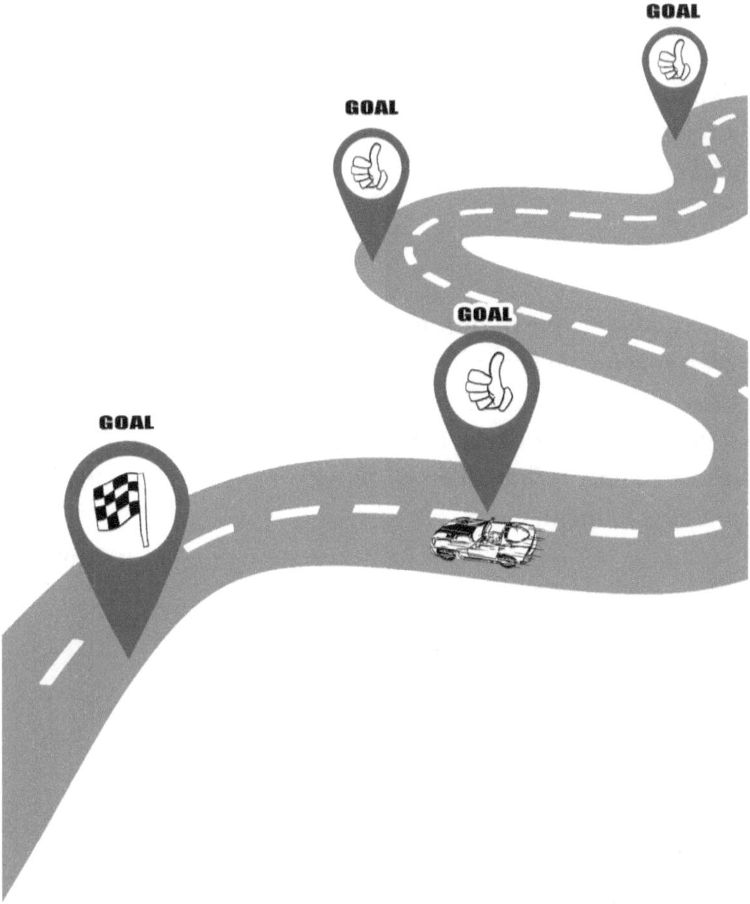

ROADMAP TO SUCCESS

'My goals have changed throughout my life. At one time it was winning awards, selling out concert dates, selling more albums than anyone else. Now, my goals are to see my grandchildren grown, live a long and healthy life with my family and friends and travel the world.'

Reba McEntire

'Successful people maintain a positive focus in life no matter what is going on around them. They stay focused on their past successes rather than their past failures, and on the next action steps they need to take to get them closer to the fulfillment of their goals rather than all the other distractions that life presents to them.'

Jack Canfield

First set the goal, next plan the route and draw the roadmap

It's as simple as that. No, seriously it is. That's really as far into the future as you need to go. Of course there will be potholes and hurdles. Don't ignore the possibility, plan for contingency, but also plan the perfect route. Be realistic about timescales but don't stretch it out so far there is no excitement reaching the milestones. Setting goals gives you something to aim for. Having a target set only just out of reach helps you maintain focus on it. If the goal is long term, setting milestones at points along the route means there are mini achievement points. Sign up for a four-year degree, fantastic. There is a start point, a roadmap, and an arrival or end point. Milestones in between may be end of year examinations, delivery of a major project, booking a holiday for the summer break, returning home during a semester break. If you expend the energy planning further than that, it will more than likely be wasted. What happens if after one year in you hate the course and want to change direction? All of the heartache about what to do after completing the degree is lost to you. So, don't set your targets too far ahead. This will also protect your mind from waves of overthinking, over-analysis and reworking.

Working life for me has centred around projects. In fact it seems most of my life has been stepping from project to project. Even as a university lecturer I ran million-dollar projects; it seems there was no escape. My personality lends itself well to project management. A project has a distinct beginning and an expected end. It's a discrete event with only the occasional chaotic intervention. Even my longest project of four years had enough milestones and decision points to maintain my interest and motivation. My natural ability to manage projects means this is how I view and live life. My goal, is my next deliverable. It has a start date, milestones and an end point. My working life must have challenge—without it I stagnate, succumb to boredom and lose motivation.

Working for the UK government for ten years with no real ladder of progression to climb up or aim for, showed me early in my career exactly what I didn't want: to be locked into mind-numbing repetitive boredom. A career and work role which does not promote personal growth is my idea of hell. Of course almost every career and job has elements of repetition. Processes, systems, shifts, tasks, schedules in the main have a timeline. Repeating these over and over again brings proficiency, skill and expertise. Moving from trainee or apprentice to master craftsman, captain, chief or executive is an aspirational path to recognition for the achievement, but it's not the only path to fulfilment. Plus, not everyone has the dream of succession. For some designing the most comfortable seating on an aircraft, writing the perfect hymn, being present at the delivery of a wild baby elephant, may be their ultimate dream. Or, selling the most cars in a month, getting all of the kids through their examinations, finding a permanent home for just one homeless person, designing a drug which eliminates a disease, welding the perfect weld. The human capacity for excellence is limitless. We are all different and therefore our goals and ambitions will all be different. The point is, **having** the goals and ambitions and working towards them.

My holidays are less about relaxation and more about adventure. The last time I laid on a beach doing nothing but reading books and heading off to the bar as soon as the sun went down, was on my first honeymoon in 1981. It was so boring I vowed to never waste oxygen doing it again (lying on a beach that is, not the honeymoon!). That's not to say I'm not a lover of beaches: it's quite the opposite, I adore them. But, there must be a purpose. We've been to some incredible beaches around the world, from Florida to the Maldives to the Solomon Islands to Guam to Queensland. I'd say however that eighty percent of those visits, were for scuba diving. The consequence of this is the planning necessary to build a monumental holiday. We choose the destination (in some cases because of the type of fish or shark we might see in the water) and plan around it. The only exception has been attending an event or a training course where the destination may be tied to the quality of the instruction or learning experience. I chose to do my divemaster qualification in Fort Lauderdale because the dive school had an international reputation. My husband chose to do his pilot's licence near Murray Bridge because the flying school had a national reputation for excellence in instruction.

Travel for my husband and I, has never been about cost. I have, and always will believe that fulfilling a goal, means making it happen. I have signed up to lengthy or difficult contracts because it provided the income to fulfil a goal. In my career every project was different. The goal was successful delivery of that project on time and within budget. Running alongside this has been the next holiday goal. Deliver a successful project, meet the criteria for the bonus, fulfil the goal of taking the adventure. This has inspired me to move from goal to goal. Less important has been setting down roots, laying the foundation for a long-term relationship with a city, town or location. I have moved around the world because I have followed the adventure dream. The dream was not looking for a home with longevity. A new home is almost an extension of the travel bug. A chance to experience a different location, town, lifestyle and community.

Without challenge, boredom seeps in and I find myself searching around for something new. New learning, new café, new jumper, new video game, new social media opportunity, new activity, new holiday destination, new sport, new flavour of gin. So it continues.

Remember there is no wrong turn. A junction is nothing more than a decision point. Which school to send the kids too? First set the goal. Type of school, location of school, distance away from home, specialist educational opportunity, cheapest school, most expensive school, boarding school, school overseas, the best education the location has to offer, the premium school for X University? Be honest with yourself about this. You're not competing with anyone else so don't fall into the trap of:

> 'Using money you haven't earned to buy things you don't need to impress people you don't like.'
> **Robert Quillen**

Made the decision? Stick with it. Or, if something comes up which has influence on the decision which was not known at the time of the decision, change it. But never, once a decision is made, ruminate over the rights and wrongs of the decision or the process. At the time the decision was taken, it was the *right decision.*

Remember that: **AT THE TIME THE DECISION WAS TAKEN, IT WAS THE RIGHT DECISION.**

We can loosely frame our lives in the form of goals. Goals can be tangible or intangible. Goals are targets, milestones, products or the realisation of dreams. Goals can be very short, short, medium and long term. To one person a goal may be getting out of bed every morning. For others it is finding a quick route in order to get the kids to school on time. Another may be meeting a deadline, or finishing a project, or passing a major exam. Having two healthy children may be a goal. Saving enough money to buy a certain coat. The list and shape of goals is endless.

Tangible Goals

It might be old but it's still relevant for **TANGIBLE** goals: **SMART** (Specific, Measurable, Achievable, Relevant and Time-bound.)

Specific: What is it that you want to accomplish? Why do you want to do it? What are the benefits of doing this? Who will be involved? Where will it happen?

Measurable: What is needed? How much is it going to cost? How will you know you've achieved it? What are you going to put in place to measure progress towards it? Where will you place the milestones?

Achievable: How are you going to achieve the goal? Does it rely on some form of action or learning or training or activity? What knowledge is needed? Do you need new skills?

Relevant: Is the goal worthwhile? It is realistic? Is this the appropriate time for the goal or are you looking too far ahead? Is there a distinct need for it?

Time-Bound: Does this goal have a start and end date? Will it be achieved more than once? Is there a timeframe in which you have to fit everything in? What will you do now to move towards the goal?

Keep the goal simple but apply **SMART** to it. Create a **GOAL STATEMENT** using the bones of the **SMART** framework.

ROADMAP TO SUCCESS

GOAL STATEMENT: I *will* go on a once in a lifetime specialist cruise to Antarctica for a minimum of eight days with a maximum budget of $20,000 before my sixtieth birthday, and I will start this project TODAY.

GOAL: I *will* take a specialist cruise to ANTARCTICA

Specific – Antarctica
Measurable – timeframe and maximum cost?
Achievable – everything is achievable if there is no barrier, think of the barriers and how they will be overcome (time, income, family, farm, pets, travel restrictions, VISA, valid passport)
Relevant – give yourself a realistic goal
Time-Bound – before 12 September 2021

GOAL: I *will* lose thirty kilos

Specific – thirty kilograms
Measurable – ½ kilo per week
Achievable – it would be easy to say 1 kilo per week but a ½ kilo each week is achievable
Relevant – reduce calorie intake, choose a keto or 5-2 diet (examples only), engage in more exercise, reduce the risk of heart disease/ diabetes (insert your biggest health fear), completely eliminate sugar
Time-Bound – set the deadline, but remember to add milestones, e.g. 20 weeks for 10 kilos

GOAL: I *will* purchase an electric car before this time next year

Specific – be precise, which electric car, make and model

Measurable – what is the total cost, including offsetting the purchase with a trade-in

Achievable – if I can get '$' as a trade-in for my existing vehicle, and that means I have to save '$' for the model I have chosen, how much do I have to earn each month in order to reach the target saved

Relevant – is the annual rego cheaper for this type of vehicle? How much will I save not having to purchase fuel? What are the servicing costs for this type of vehicle? Will I achieve a better resale value for this type of vehicle? What are the insurance cost implications? How will I charge the vehicle when I am at work?

Time-Bound – set the deadline date with milestones for achieving savings of '$' in the bank every quarter

Set the goal in a positive framework. You *will* do something, you *will* achieve a degree, you *will* become a journalist.

Set priorities. The goal is worth achieving so make sure the planning is exceptional. Imprinting the goal and its stages in the mind helps to imprint the finished achievement. Research, research and more research firms up the goal from an idea to milestones. How will you get to Antarctica? Does the chosen tour company include flights or are they to be purchased and booked separately? Are you good at planning trips yourself or do you need to enlist the help of an agent? Set the milestones in stone. Calculate the costs down to the bus fare to the airport and be honest with yourself. If you don't want to fly economy don't factor in economy priced flights. If you don't want to sleep in a bunk room with three strangers don't factor in the cheapest cabin price. If you want more than eating in fast food restaurants on a budget of $10 per day, set real targets. Everything is achievable, it just takes realism, motivation, commitment and sensible careful planning.

Reminder: life goes on regardless. The goal may be so exciting, pursuing it may absorb much of your time and energy. Don't forget everything else. Family, work and other commitments need to keep going in parallel to pursuit of the goals.

Intangible Goals

Intangible things have no obvious physical form. Some examples of this may be how many skills you have, your emotions, how much knowledge you have, how wise you are, your values, your communication skills, your experience, your ideas and your thoughts. In business intangible things could be brand, trade secrets, intellectual property and data, and workplace culture.

SMART is simply not good enough for the setting of intangible goals—they are subjective and open to individual scrutiny and interpretation and can be potentially quite woolly. For example, how do you set achievable milestones for having no regrets? Or what about spending more time with family? How would that be measured? If your goal is intangible try to turn it into a tangible goal. For example instead of spending more time with the family what does that look like? Do you want to spend more time with the kids, parents, grandparents, cousins? How often do you want to see them? Do you want to set aside specific times each week/ month to physically spend time with them? Are they remote, can you set up a video call on set days and times? It's similar to the goal of losing weight. Unless timeframes and actual kilos are added, stating losing weight doesn't mean very much, so construct a framework of tangible goals.

Now that you're turning all of your intangible goals into tangible goals, there should only be ONE intangible goal left: to **ELIMINATE NEGATIVITY**. Master this and anything is possible.

Ultimately you will need to address what it is you really want from your life. Everyone is different. Not everyone has a burning goal to jump out of an aircraft, some people would just like to be able to breastfeed their child, jog a kilometre, cook a perfect boiled egg or pass a test. We are all different. We all face different challenges and therefore have different goals. Also remember that goals morph and change as we pass through stages of our life.

List **THREE TANGIBLE GOALS**, write a **GOAL STATEMENT** for each one, and then use **SMART** for each goal to define and refine the detail of the goal.

List **THREE INTANGIBLE GOALS** (remember they are difficult to quantify) and for each one, define and refine precisely what they are. Find a way to flip the intangible goal into a **TANGIBLE GOAL**.

ENGINE'S ROAR

YOUR LAST SELF-HELP BOOK

'You gain strength, courage, and confidence by every experience in which you really stop to look fear in the face. You are able to say to yourself, "I lived through this horror. I can take the next thing that comes along." '

Eleanor Roosevelt

'Your time is limited, so don't waste it living someone else's life. Don't be trapped by dogma—which is living with the results of other people's thinking. Don't let the noise of others' opinions drown out your own inner voice. And most important, have the courage to follow your heart and intuition.'

Steve Jobs

In order to achieve balance in your life, you must **ELIMINATE NEGATIVITY**, and this is now your number one goal. This isn't the same as thinking positively. It is virtually impossible to eradicate negative thoughts but it is possible to flip a negative thought into a positive outcome. The mind is conditioned to problem solve and analyse and with this comes negativity.

- I've tried not thinking about the negative thought – **FAILED**.
- I've tried to completely block out the negative thought – **FAILED**.
- I've tried to look at the negative thought in a more positive light – **FAILED**.

The architect of most of your woes it could be said, is ***negativity***.

To help you, let's start with **MEMORY MODULES**.

Apply to university, or stay in well-paid employment in a dead-end job? Most of my thoughts were in the negative. What if I don't like university? Everyone will be younger than me—what if this becomes a barrier? What if I'm not smart enough? My maths is rusty what if I can't keep up? How am I going to survive on the student grant, paying the rent and all of the bills, affording childcare and buying text books? What if, what if, what if! What if all of those things could be taken care of, then what? Well, my mind would still automatically try and find something negative to dwell on.

It took three more months of stalling and arguing with myself to make the leap. Another three months waiting for confirmation I had been accepted onto the course, and another three months before my notice period was fulfilled and then the first day of the course approached. At the point where I handed in my notice, this was the perceived point of no return. As if the only choice open to me now was the course when in reality with my experience and skills, I could have applied for other jobs and no doubt would have been successful. I would say my natural instinct veered towards risk aversion but I know this can't be true, given my sheer delight at jumping out of aircraft and skydiving back to earth. In truth, having jumped off towers and bungee jumped off platforms, I have no doubt my fear gene has either evolved, or is completely missing.

With a different and more positive approach the negative barriers could have been flipped to:

- University will be fantastic and I'll get free access to (insert favourite free activity, e.g. library, technology, student life).
- Age is just a number and I mix well with all generations.
- I've met the entry criteria so it's going to be a fabulous learning journey.
- I'll ask about extra maths and learning support if I feel I'm struggling with some of the concepts.
- I will check out the childcare facilities at the college.
- If I rent closer to the campus that will save on travel costs.
- I don't need to buy all of the text books, the library has long-term loan arrangements.

Looking back now on my years at university, they were incredible. Everyone gelled well, there was a culture of peer support, childcare was free for single parents, travel was free for students, the library was extremely well stocked, computing access was free, and the student learning support was exemplary. My differential equations may have been a bit on the flaky side to start with but it didn't take me long with support to fly high. Free travel meant the need to relocate was eliminated, it just required reducing expenditure to fit in with the small budget available to me.

The extraordinary beauty of diving is the weightlessness. The diver adds air to the buoyancy compensation jacket (BCD) on to which the scuba tank is attached. Out of the water the equipment is heavy and cumbersome, but once underwater the naturally buoyant seawater coupled with the BCD allows the diver to simulate complete weightlessness. This feeling alone instils a deep sense of serenity. The same feeling I experience when concentrating on the road during a motorbike ride. The same feeling a skydive creates. The mind is absorbed in the activity. Concentration is absolute. All of these activities involve preservation of life. There is little room for error. High speed riding requires awareness of surroundings, the machine and observation of everything while scanning for potential hazards. Diving requires constant attention to depth, air usage, gas absorption and time underwater. Skydiving requires perfect physical attitude to the earth so as not to spin or fall out of control, and a close watch of the altimeter to ensure the parachute is deployed at the correct opening height. There are emergency procedures for skydiving and scuba diving which are learned during extensive training and are drilled in through repetitive practice. While the mind devotes itself to such high levels of concentration there is no room for frivolous thinking. This is perhaps one reason why I have always been drawn to intensive extreme sports. They all block pointless thought and reflection, in favour of survival and life.

ENGINE'S ROAR

My first night dive was on a reef wall. Apart from the torches each diver was pointing at parrot fish hiding their heads in their mucus bubbles of air, or shining them at the myriad of fish tucked into every coral nook and cranny, the ocean was in pitch blackness. It can be quite disconcerting to turn and face the black ocean behind. No matter how the eye strains to find an image or a shape there is nothing but complete silent blackness. My husband Chris is less of a fan of night diving than I am. There is something enveloping about black water, something soothing like a giant hug. For Chris it is more about what he can't see in the darkness. The ocean after all is filled with the unknown, and with sharks. Most of the hundreds of sharks we have encountered are quite harmless, but there are two or three types with well-deserved fearsome reputations. Our very first close encounter was on this first night dive. We had been happily hanging around the reef wall for a good fifteen minutes when I felt a firm and insistent tap on the shoulder and then a finger pointing to my right. A blacktip reef shark of about two metres in length was swimming along the wall at my eye level, straight towards me. I admired its sleek perfect beauty. Its effortless sway as it swam towards me. I was fascinated and I simply stayed as motionless as possible so as not to miss a moment. Chris however was not too keen on the unknown. He had been hovering alongside me but as the shark drew closer my instinct told me he was less than comfortable. At this point he placed his hands on my shoulders and effectively placed me in-between himself and the shark. As the shark came closer a myriad of small black dots on its nose became visible. Yes it was that close. These are the ampullae of Lorenzini, the electroreceptor sensing organs filled with jelly which sense electrical fields in the water. The shark detects as it swims. It detects danger, it detects food, it detects its environment. So of course it was going to detect me and less than a metre away from me it veered away at lightning speed. I am human, I am a predator, of course it swam off. It is a moment in time which has and will stay with me in perfect detail until the day I die.

This is a **MEMORY MODULE**. A positive moment which can be given a distinct purpose. The original memory stays intact, its detail is clear and never changes. It is a captured moment in time, from a beautiful holiday. I use the bones of the memory however, for other purposes. I refer to it as a ***shark attack***.

Have you ever been in a meeting where you are constrained by position or professionalism and cannot say what you want to say? Perhaps someone is verbally swinging wildly at your role, your work, your ethics, or your political or religious choices. As a respectful person, or because of the culture or environment you find yourself in, shouting and screaming across the table to correct this person would not be seen as good form. So you sit in silence like a slowly boiling pot, ready to blow the lid right off the disrespect. As anger and pressure build you focus closely on the face of the negative person. Focus, focus, focus. Now start the shark attack. Imagine the shark, any type and size of shark that you like, appearing in the distance behind this person. You can see the extraordinary beauty of the perfectly formed shark as it sleekly slides closer. Closer and closer it swims, its powerful tail propelling it forward in silence. Now, I'll leave the outcome to your imagination. Of course it doesn't have to be a shark, it can be a bear, a wolf or an enormous eagle.

A different type of **MEMORY MODULE** involves the creation of a reality substitute. In other words, not something which you have experienced, but something which you imagine. During counselling I was given a technique to practice, to reduce anxiety. It is a powerful and clever technique which can be applied in many scenarios. This **MEMORY MODULE** I refer to as ***back in the box***. The technique involves diminishing the importance of a person. Imagine the person sitting or standing where you would normally place them in your mind. Now imagine them shrinking, diminishing, reducing in size all the way down to a five-centimetre box. Now, slam the lid shut. I gave my box a colour. I chose pink which in my mind if worn by a man represents to me flowery, effeminate, fragile. Imagine the box with the person shrunk inside it sitting in the chair where the person sits, or on the floor by the desk. Now stamp on it (in your mind of course). Yes, squash it firmly underfoot, remember to twist the ball of your shoe as you would if you were extinguishing a burning cigarette. You may need to close your eyes to fully visualise the scene. Remember to have a subtle grin to yourself when the person is firmly **back in the box**.

Memories which float in the mind and all too often come forward need a different type of **MEMORY MODULE**. When the mind has revisited events or incidents or issues or problems enough, which we need to do in order to find closure, or where there is a feeling that rumination is debilitating and little is gained from revisiting them, it is time to send them backwards in the mind. Lying in bed at night when there is silence and darkness, and we just can't fall asleep without revisiting something just one more time, should bring forward a method of shutting the thoughts down. This **MEMORY MODULE** I refer to as the *curtain call*. We ruminate over unsettled or unresolved items. They stay in the mind and we cannot put them to bed, figuratively. My solution is to send the thought backwards to the back of my mind, to a parking area I call the **toolbox**, which exists behind a set of dark scarlet velvet curtains. The memory is placed inside a drawer in the **toolbox**. If the memory or image is particularly distressing, it is sent to the bottom drawer. It requires a conscious effort to close the drawer. The **toolbox** resembles a mechanic's multi-drawer chest and is located in a darkened corner of the memory garage. Once the image or thought is locked in the drawer, I pull down a zipper on my imaginary velvet curtains. The pull tab on the zipper is made of solid gold and the zip itself has large gold teeth, and makes a distinct zipping sound as it is drawn downwards. This locks the thought firmly in the **toolbox**, and there it stays. When I consign something to the **toolbox** it rarely reappears. It is a conscious effort to keep it in the drawer and the bottom drawer is reserved for the items I have ruminated over sometimes for years not months. It has been a controlled effort over many years to create the drawer structure, and the velvet curtains. I highly recommend this method. It isn't something which can be simply created, it takes time and repetition, but it does work.

Create **MEMORY MODULES** using your own experiences or preferences. They may need to come from your own imagination so they are easier to recall. Of primary importance is the imagery which allows you to shut down, or shut out, recurring negative or upsetting thoughts. If my memory modules resonate with you, feel free to use them.

You will need **THREE** effective and easily recalled **MEMORY MODULES**:

- A module which stops a thought dead (shark attack).
- A module in which you can slam the door shut (back in the box).
- A module which can quickly immobilise (curtain call) a thought, but which may then use a second memory module to be more effective (the toolbox).

LIMITLESS

YOUR LAST SELF-HELP BOOK

'For a lot of people, Superman is and has always been America's hero. He stands for what we believe is the best within us: limitless strength tempered by compassion, that can bear adversity and emerge stronger on the other side. He stands for what we all feel we would like to be able to stand for, when standing is hardest.'

J. Michael Straczynski

'But I think it's more that when you're young, you're invincible, you're immortal—or at least you think you are. The possibilities are limitless, you're inventing the future. Then you get older and suddenly you have a history. It's fixed. You can't change anything. I find that a bit disturbing, to be honest.'

Damien Hirst

How can you move past your limiting beliefs to become **LIMITLESS?**

Believe in yourself. Believe in your abilities. Don't let anyone stamp on your dreams. If you can dream it, you can do it. If you've already been practising creating **MEMORY MODULES**, you've begun the visualisation journey. What you want to do however, is visualise in the positive, not the negative. Do not creep back into that deep pit where you constantly relive and rehearse negative actions or activities. Your visualisation must be creative, not reflective.

- o   Visualise the home of your dreams in every detail. Create your perfect bathroom in your mind, feel the softness of the towels, the warmth of the underfloor heating, the sun streaming in through the clear glass windows.

- Visualise the perfect kitchen. The up-market appliances. The stone benchtops and wide range hood.

- Visualise your next holiday. The sun-kissed beach, the azure blue of the ocean, sitting in the chair on the deck of the cabin looking out to sea.

- Visualise the perfect career. Sitting in the manager's chair in an oak-lined office. Standing in the courtroom delivering a world-beating closing argument. Handing over a certificate of excellence to the one hundredth student passing their driving test.

Visualisation helps to crystallise goals. I often think back to the age-old argument about which came first, the mind of the creative writer or the science. Was the fiction based on fact, or was it the other way around? Jules Verne's *From the Earth to the Moon* being a wonderful example of this enigma. There's a good reason the genre is named Science Fiction. The idea lends itself greatly to dream it, then do it. Create the image in the most intricate of detail in the mind, and then build the plan to turn the fiction into fact and reality. Isn't that to some degree what we all do? We derive a path, a need, a want and we focus on it, to either actively pursue it, or inactively keep dreaming about it.

Did you predict the future? Imagine the future? Create the future through visualisation? How often have you been in a situation where you think to yourself:

- 'I've been here before'
- 'I've dreamt of this happening'
- 'I've predicted this would happen'.

They are our déjà vu moments and through our lives we may experience dozens of them. There are many theories for how and why déjà vu occurs, some firmly footed in logic and science while others, including alien abduction and reincarnation, simply the domain of the surreal. I started this book with the fact the human brain is probably the most complex structure in the universe and as a result, it's full capacity may never be known. It should be said that finding out why déjà vu occurs is probably not at the forefront of neuroscience, however, don't let that stop you from using intense and consistent visualisation to rewire your thoughts.

I had an interesting discussion once with an evolutionary biologist about rewiring memories to make them more palatable. We were both attending a conference in Melbourne, Australia and the odd topic of giving robots fake memories so they could begin to put situations into a context based on experiential memory came up. As we worked around the subject, the idea of 'why don't we do this now with everyday thoughts?' came about. Indeed, why don't we? Or do we already do this without thinking about it? Do we inadvertently sugar-coat our memories to make them more palatable? If we do, at what point does the replacement memory become the enduring memory, and at what point does the precision of the actual memory fade and is lost? If we have the ability to selectively replace the memory then perhaps we should be doing it more often with those memories we don't want to remember in their current form. Then there is a question of how much should we alter in order to either retain something of the original, yet alter enough to make it more palatable presents itself.

My memories of the abuse at school is less about the physical details of the abuser and more about the environmental factors. His kipper ties, tight crimplene trousers, 1970s aftershave, hair flap combed over his bald patch. How that must have dented his image. The make and colour of his car. Where he lived. But I cannot tell you about the depth of his voice, the colour of his eyes, the shape of his mouth or anything else about his facial or more obvious physical features. I remember the inside of the history class store cupboard and the floor to ceiling shelves filled with blank exercise books, pens and pencils, text books and boxes of chalk. I have no idea of wall colour or the type of flooring. I remember distinctly the threatening words he spoke.

In writing these paragraphs, memories I placed long ago in the bottom drawer of the **toolbox** behind the scarlet velvet curtains, have been released from long-term storage. It has not been a pleasant experience; but the book is a journey in repositioning of hardened negative memories, and the effectiveness of the mind tools I have created to rearrange, order, delete and overshadow them.

When we try and remember, consciously work through a memory in order to arrive at, let's say a date when something happened, the route we take is in reverse order. It is easier to work backwards, to use other milestones and events in order to position the memory in its correct location in time. How many times have you tried to work out when something happened by aligning it with a birth, the first day at school, when did we move to X town and so on? Can we **REVERSE ENGINEER** a memory? Can we alter the specifics so that how we remember it in future is through an altered state? To reverse engineer anything, we must reduce it to its component parts. Let's be more specific. This is about altering conscious remembered memory, not attempting any form of genetic manipulation or alteration to unconscious processes.

At school I was abused in a number of different locations, but mostly inside the history class store cupboard. At one point when asked to fetch something from another store cupboard in a different classroom learning a different subject, I refused. This added to my growing reputation for delinquency which often resulted in pages and pages of lines being awarded to me for my poor behaviour. Nevertheless, I was not about to enter into any cupboard where a teacher was present in the room, regardless of how many students were also present in the room. The threat was removed once I left school. The memory remained. At some point I consciously decided to close the literal door on the whole experience and this is how **REVERSE ENGINEERING** began for me. In my mind I retraced my steps to the point where each instance would begin. Sometimes mid-class, sometimes after class, sometimes under the disguise of tidying up the cupboard. I wonder how many others in any given week would be tidying up the cupboard!

School was over and done with, repetition was impossible so why not close the literal door on the whole sordid event. When the memory resurfaced I allowed it to replay. Forcing whichever instance I was thinking about to begin at the beginning. When I arrived at the store cupboard door, the key could not be located. No matter how much fumbling in jacket or trouser pockets was done, the key had simply gone missing and the door remained locked, holding inside the cupboard, the part of the memory I did not want to revisit. As the years rolled by the dark wood of the door became the memory. The detail was all but lost, and remains lost. You cannot alter the past, but you can manipulate the memory so remembering it is no longer the place of despair it once was.

Now, I can hear some of you screaming out loud about facing the memory, challenging it, overcoming it and moving forward in the face of it. Yes, all true and all good tactics. But there is also a point where we need to move past it. We have ruminated over it, revisited it, questioned it, challenged it, screamed at it, cried over it again and again until we are almost broken by it. Once we have done all of these things we arrive at the reckoning point where we say stop, enough is enough, it's time to **REVERSE ENGINEER** this memory. It is not going to have any kind of hold on me for a second longer. This is the visual reference point, where the memory changes direction, changes shape, is **REVERSE ENGINEERED.**

Let's revisit what may be limiting you. 'I am not (insert limiting belief) enough'. Maybe, thin enough, pretty, tall, fat, happy, skilled, professional, valued, smart, rich, poor and many more *enoughs*. All of these are personal judgements of self-worth. By what are you measuring these? You don't have a Ferrari in the garage and therefore you're not rich enough! Your dress size is 18 so you're not thin enough! You only just passed the examination so clearly you can't be qualified enough! Right? Wrong. Did you study to be a doctor? No, then you are not a doctor. Are you bright enough to be a doctor? Have you applied to do a qualification which would result in a career as a doctor? Yes, and you did not achieve pass marks? It does not mean you are not bright enough to be a doctor, it means you didn't achieve a pass in those examinations. Did you study enough in preparation for those examinations? If you believe you can't, you won't. It used to be said that failed doctors became pharmacists. How many qualified pharmacists do you personally know? Exactly, not many.

Instead of assuming you're not X enough, analyse what it is you want to achieve. *I'm not thin enough*! Thin enough for what? As a size 18 no, you won't fit into a size 14 dress. Do you want to fit into a size 14 dress? Yes. Have you designed a weight realignment program for yourself?

I'm not smart enough! Smart enough to do what? Smart enough to race a supercar? Smart enough to work on the checkout at the supermarket? Smart enough to write a bestselling novel? First define smart. If smart means having a degree well, go and study for one.

I'm not valued enough! What is being valued, what does it mean for you? You want to be important? You want to be of benefit to others? You want to be recognised for being an amazing friend? What does being important mean? How do you want to be of benefit to others? What are you doing which requires special friendship recognition?

We are all different and as a result we all have a different view of the world and of others, and of how we fit into the world. But to self-limit what and who we are, is to restrict our potential and confine our abilities.

I don't have enough money for X! It's the easiest and most used excuse on the planet. Guess what? It's an excuse for *I can't be bothered to work towards my goal so I'll tell myself I just don't have the money*.

When I lived in Scotland a couple of close friends decided to take a year to travel around the world before they married and started a family. They were in debt up to their eyeballs with a mortgage and apartment they should never have bought and three credit cards constantly nudging their maximum allowable balance. The car was either in the workshop or in the garage for lack of money for repairs or for fuel. Yet both of them were on relatively high annual salaries. The desire to travel around the world seemed to get further and further away. I had purchased a one-bedroom starter home which was barely big enough to swing a cat in. I commuted to work on a motorbike and read books from the library. My one great love of the time was my games machine but I was so bad at adventure and fantasy games it took me six months to work my way through them and then I purchased pre-owned versions.

After many conversations about goals and how to achieve them their limiting beliefs were changed for limitless ambitions. The apartment was put on the market and as the real estate climate was in a climb they sold quickly, realising their asking price. They moved into rented accommodation on a twelve-month lease. After paying off two credit cards and the mortgage they still had eighteen thousand pounds on the other card to clear. Instead of dining out four or five times per week they dined out on Saturdays. They sold the car with one of them able to use public transport and the other investing in a second hand scooter. They stopped wasting money on expensive clothing working their way through box loads of unworn clothes they had purchased but never worn. They sold appliances which had sat in cupboards in the kitchen having never been used, and downsized their oversized life in preparation for travel. They went from a crowded, overfilled lifestyle to minimal. They had a schedule and a leaving date. Once the final credit card was clear they booked round the world tickets and this locked in their leaving date. It was an open-ended ticket with up to fifteen different stopovers which was just as well, as their year turned into three! They lodged five-thousand pounds with their parents for emergencies and left the UK with five-thousand in travel money. Both of them had computing and technology backgrounds and while the first six months were hard, more for being away from

LIMITLESS

everything they had known as dependable and safe, a lack of money never hindered them at all. They would find two or three months of work, save enough for an adventure, move on and then stop to earn some more. Twenty-six countries and thirty-eight months later they returned to Scotland to a wedding they'd planned while in Moscow, and career changes for both of them. They never returned to their wasteful lifestyle and found time for at least two adventures per year even with three children.

Limiting beliefs are just that, beliefs. Once you remove the belief there is nothing but **you**, stopping **you** from moving towards **your** goals. If you believe your life can be limitless, it will be limitless. Being limitless means focusing on moving forward. No-one suggests it is quick or easy. Being limitless means making it happen.

Visualise what you ultimately want, do not be limited in your goals, **BE LIMITLESS.**

Do you now know who you are? Do you now know what you can become? Are you setting one goal at a time?

- Can you recognise your **EVOLUTIONARY MOMENTS**?
- Are you ready to **ACTIVATE CHANGE** or **ACTIVATE GROWTH**?
- Are you armed and ready to **ELIMINATE NEGATIVITY**?
- Have you created **MEMORY MODULES** which are personal to your life, your activities, your circumstances, your experiences?
- Are you able to **VISUALISE**?
- Can you **REVERSE ENGINEER** your memories?
- Have you moved past your limiting beliefs to become **LIMITLESS**?

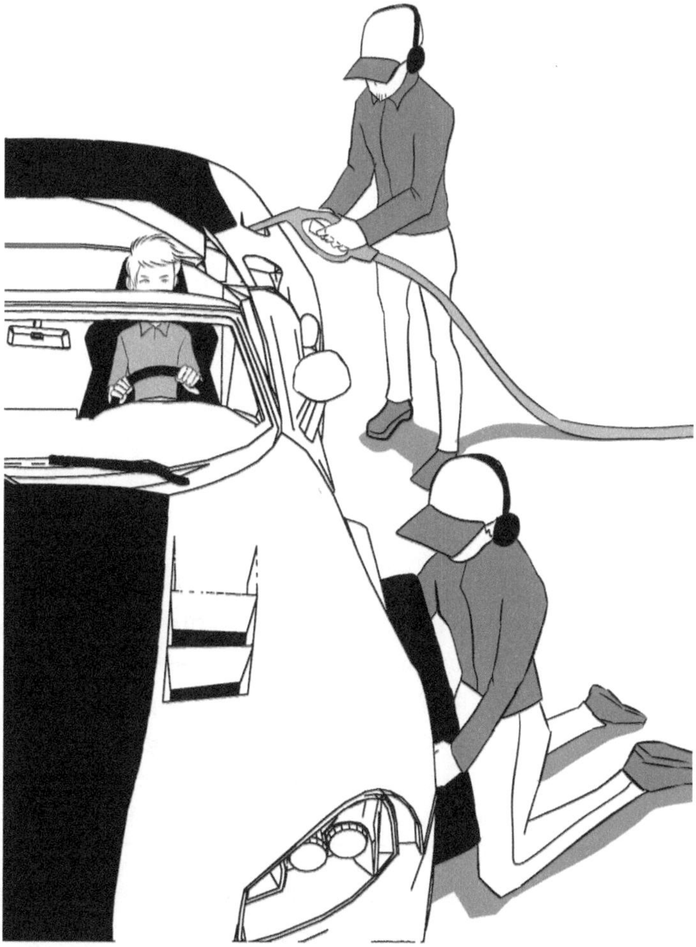

PIT CREW

'At the end of the day, life is about being happy being who you are, and I feel like we are so blessed to have the support system and the best family to really just support each other no matter what we're going through.'

Kim Kardashian

'To enjoy good health, to bring true happiness to one's family, to bring peace to all, one must first discipline and control one's own mind. If a man can control his mind he can find the way to Enlightenment, and all wisdom and virtue will naturally come to him.'

Buddha

How much support is available to you? I'm certain it's more than you realise. We naturally look to family and friends to support us, but their support is not always available or possible. Just because people do not want to, or cannot support you, does not mean your goals are to be derailed. Support comes in many forms. Never push support to one side and if you need it, actively seek it out. Your support will be your changing **PIT CREW**. I refer to it as the **PIT CREW** because people and services will move in and out of the support model. When we are at school we are supported by teaching staff but when we move on to a college, the support changes. As we change jobs or change careers, the support model also changes.

People move in and out of our lives, throughout our lives. We build relationships with people and grow as a result of them. Life is however in perpetual motion. Leverage the best support that you can at the time when you need it. While it is often a challenge and not always easy this means *eliminating negative people*. Now, I know what you're thinking! My (insert family member) is (insert relationship to you), how am I supposed to eliminate them from my life? Sometimes we have to create a closed loop for that person. They exist almost in a bubble. What happens in the bubble is confined to the bubble.

Negative people are draining. If you have a negative voice in a position of influence at work, it can affect the productivity of the whole organisation. Eliminating them is difficult and often impossible especially if you are not in a role to which they directly report. If it is impractical for you to request a move to a different department or to under a different management structure, it might be best to seek out a different employer. I know, easy to say and hard to action, however, when the negativity begins to affect your mental health, it is time for real change.

Negative people are everywhere. Walk away from them. No seriously, walk away from them. How many times have you been in conversation at work, at school, at college, as a parent watching the kids play sport, in a meeting, sitting at a restaurant table, waiting for a train, sitting on a bus, sitting on a plane, in a stadium, at a concert, at the movies, and all you can hear is someone, or a group of people moaning and complaining about something or someone. If you are involved in the conversation, try something new... *I'm sorry but if you're going to continue to be this negative about (insert name, place, article, item), I'm afraid you'll have to continue this discussion without me.* If you are not involved in the conversation place headphones in your ears (on a plane), change seats (bus or train), change tables, move to a different free seat at the stadium, in fact, simply get out of earshot. The conversation will draw you downwards, out of a positive frame of mind, into a negative mindset. Get used to saying *I'm going to stop you there*, then walk away.

Gossip serves no purpose whatsoever. It is one or more person's opinion, often lacking depth or substance, used to influence or deflect. Walk away from gossip and innuendo, there is no positivity inside the gossip thread. The content has not been thought about, and no deep thinking or insight is contained within it. Are you the subject of the gossip? Walk away from it. They are gossiping because they cannot break into your inner circle so instead, they are constructing an alternative to reality and basically making up anything which fits their purpose. Challenging them is a waste of energy, uses up valuable oxygen you will need to pursue something more exciting, and gives a tiny bit of credibility to their fictional creation. Remember the reason they are gossiping is they have nothing of depth to talk about. Those who gossip always end up on the conversation table themselves as nothing more than annoyances. When eventually they do have something of interest to impart people rarely listen. As you walk away reflect on your achievement by inwardly affirming your actions:

- o   Words cannot harm me
- o   I do not need to listen to their rubbish
- o   Those people are not in my inner circle
- o   I am strong, bold, honest and true.

Affirmations are your instant positive bullets which shoot down negative vibes. You can use them all day, every day. Use them in challenging situations, or moments of high stress.

Many times in my life I have been before video cameras and occasionally live television. Whether for the recording of lectures broadcast as part of live lecture delivery, or recorded as part of specific course or module content for delivery on demand. Lectures are often recorded in one take, and while editing is possible where they are delivered on demand, live broadcast is often much more nerve-racking. One of my peers taught me a valuable lesson very early in my lecturing career. When in front of the camera or lecture theatre filled with students and a room full of eager faces, remember to concentrate on breathing normally, and always say at least half a dozen positive affirmations before beginning the lecture:

- o   I am calm
- o   I am an excellent speaker

PIT CREW

- o   I am an expert in my subject
- o   I am confident
- o   I am well prepared
- o   I am authentic

… and repeat them until ready to start speaking. Take a deep breath, and begin. It is natural to have breaks in speech, take a deep breath and keep moving forward in subject matter. Your notes need to be minimal. Your slides loaded with bullet points not paragraphs. You know your subject, you can deliver it easily, and there isn't a question you cannot answer.

Now repeat for a managerial address, presentation, TED talk, keynote speech, after dinner speech or any formal or informal gathering where the focus is on you.

Now imagine the same for conversations with family, and with friends. Yes, there is a little more leverage with family who would love you unconditionally, but that doesn't mean they can take advantage of your good demeanour and negatively attack your choice of car, partner, holiday, clothing, tree, dinner, beer or anything else. Family input does not give automatic access to free shots at the coconut shy. Put your foot down if you feel too much negativity is directed at you from family and friends by simply stating 'stop', I don't need or want this kind of negativity from people close to me. Believe me, it is enough to derail the conversation and make people think about what they are talking about. Most often people don't realise what they are saying and need a simple reminder that they are travelling down a path which is neither pleasant nor constructive for them or for you.

A major problem arises when your partner has a tendency to tip toward the dark side of negativity. I am married to a retired police officer. As a career, policing cannot be classified as a positive role (by definition). Yes, there is the odd cat requiring rescue out of the tree, and returning Grandma from her unexpected walk in the park but 99% of the time, policing sits firmly in the domain of bad news.

Some careers steer personalities from the positive to the negative. It is not to say the career should be avoided, it shouldn't. Imagine the negativity nurses must endure (although it must be stated, not all of the time), and if everyone steered to the positive curve in favour of taking up a career in nursing well, we'd all be in serious trouble. There is no way you can flip the sudden death of an incoming trauma patient to a positive experience. The death of the patient is negative. No matter what happened before or after they arrived in the nursing department, these few moments before death are the most important. This is where the negative becomes the positive. Without the nurse using their skills to comfort and assist this patient, they would not have had safe passage to their end of life.

- o My training brought them to this place of final relaxation.
- o My skills enabled me to ensure this person passed without pain.
- o My presence ensured I was there to comfort this person in their final moments.

You may fight for life, you may work hard to preserve the last moments and breaths of life, and the reward is knowing you were there in those moments. This is the key to flipping a negative situation into a positive experience. You recognise the negativity, but understand your position in easing individual end of life pain (in this example). Not a simple task, not always successful, but the only way to deal with consistent and recurrent traumatic events. It should also be noted that there is no substitute for professional counselling. Counsellors are equipped to help people in high-stress employment environments work through what they have witnessed or had to deal with in a way which fits them as individuals.

Your friends are also important—make them feel important. Do you know how uplifting it is to greet a friend with a hug, kiss on the cheek or simply a loud and smiling hello? By greeting them and treating them positively, the welcome triggers a positive get together. People reflect back the demeanour they meet. They may be with you to convey something negative, where an excited and happy welcome would need to be tempered. We all have to engage in difficult and upsetting conversations but the key is to pick out the positive items. Remembering someone for the good they did, or the wonderful acts they performed, the dedication they portrayed, always looking for the joy rather than the sadness. It takes time and practice but the result will be everyone takes the warmth away and not the coldness.

Positivity breeds positivity—sadly negativity breeds negativity. Walking into a conversation which has a negative tone, attracts further negative conversation. Your goal is to flip the tone to positive.

- o **NEGATIVE:** How come that person always gets the best projects to work on and we're left with the rest?
    - o **FLIP:** We should ask that person her key tips for landing better quality projects.

- o **NEGATIVE:** Someone should tell her she looks ludicrous in that dress, she needs to find clothes which suit her age!
    - o **FLIP:** I hope you don't mind me saying but I've admired your beautiful hair for some time. I think you'd look good in this style, it's got classy lines and is made for your style of cut.

- o **NEGATIVE:** It doesn't matter how many times I tell that idiot to line up the tins, they still get it wrong.
    - o **FLIP:** Hi, I've noticed you're having difficulty working out the best way to display the tins, can I show you what I think?

While we are on the subject of **flipping** the negative to the positive, let's spend some time on **assumptions**. We can make negative and positive assumptions but the ones which do the damage are negative. As we age we seem to make less assumptions, basing our comments and decisions more on learned experience and facts. When we are younger we fill in the unknowns with assumptions, and it is one of the most dangerous activities we perform. Getting the assumption wrong can damage our credibility, our reputations, our careers and career aspirations, our relationships, friendships and professional status.

I was recently targeted for expressing an interest in a vegan activist activity which had taken place in Adelaide, South Australia. The activists had attended a gathering where a whole professionally prepared butchered animal was on a spit roast. The activists made a silent protest holding up banners. My interest in the article was the fact the activists who were standing in silence were asked to leave the public park. This in my mind was a suggestion freedom to speak or protest was being eroded. In the same month some more progressive activists had trespassed onto farms around the nation, trying to bring to mainstream attention their claims around treatment of farm animals. The article appeared in print and on social media and I retweeted the article and quoted the comments made by the person leading the silent protest. A local person took aim at the repost either misinterpreting its written content and or the quoted comments, throwing an amazing attack in my direction suggesting I was a vegan, I was supporting the activism, and had attended the actual silent protest. The assumptions had far reaching effects. The first was to link me directly to a protest I had not attended, and also to suggest I was a vegan which I am not. The subsequent attack on social media could have been said to have damaged my reputation. I support our local farming community and I keep farm animals myself. This attack now painted me in a poor light and could suggest I was being hypocritical in supporting the activism while also keeping my own farm animals. Eventually the negative comments against me were withdrawn. Not before I had paid for legal advice, and not before a large number of people had read the offensive comments against me. The lesson here is to research the facts, even down to reading the original article or content before jumping to an ill-informed conclusion. I am a vegetarian but not a vegan.

The reason I became vegetarian is that in 1996 my gall bladder was removed. As a result, with reduced bile pumped into the liver, I have spent the subsequent years fighting the biliousness and pain caused by eating red meat. During pregnancy my craving was for milk. I drank litres and litres of it every day for months. This caused a build-up of calcium which manifested as two large gall stones three centimetres in diameter. When one became lodged at the edge of the bile tube which feeds bile into the liver, the gall bladder became infected, swollen and eventually burst. I was admitted to emergency by ambulance with touch and go surgery. The scarring and damage to my digestive system has resulted in over two decades of dietary issues, and an inability to eat large quantities of protein. Eventually I resolved to simply not eat what caused me the pain and became a vegetarian. I still enjoy fish, shellfish and to some extent dairy in small amounts, and now there are large volumes of pea protein available in powder form, I can finally say I'm eating a balanced and healthy diet.

There are a number of damaging assumptions here, some of which could be that all vegans are activists, all activists attend protests, all vegans are against farming of animals, all vegans are only vegans because they dislike farming practices, and no doubt there are many more assumptions which can be added to the list. I can prove the reason for my surgery along with the numerous medications I have taken over the years. So a warning. Be certain of the facts before stating the claim.

An inaccurate assumption can lead to getting stuck on the roundabout. Being unable to challenge, depending on the circumstances, leads to the rumination around the claim or assumption. Here we are back inside our own minds conjuring up numerous ways to seek revenge or overturn the comments. It's not a good place to be. We can waste time or oxygen confronting the author of the assumption, or we can let it go. As intelligent people we simply hate injustice. Herein lies the problem. The only real way to achieve justice is confrontation, or a legal challenge. If the behaviours against someone are consistent and ongoing there will certainly be a case for a legal challenge. If this is a one-off instance then it will be better for your own mental health to **ELIMINATE NEGATIVITY** and let it go. This may mean the entire incident needs to be placed in the **toolbox** and given a *curtain call*.

We make assumptions every day. I made an assumption that my partner was open and honest with me, never thinking he could have a secret habit of dressing up in women's clothes. The local supermarket has advertised opening hours so when we turn up during those hours we assume it will be open. We assume the coffee we purchase from our favourite coffee shop will taste the same each time we drink it. We assume patterns will repeat and behaviours will endure. We make assumptions based on habits, because as human beings we prefer habits to variations.

We can also assume that our advice is wanted. Encourage people to absorb quality advice and discard ill-founded recommendations. The enlightened disperse advice leanly. They present the advice with background so that the listener understands the advice has sound foundations and is not just opinion or hot air.

During a recent election campaign a candidate was heard to state, *'What does he know about politics? He's just a farmer, you're better off voting for me'*. Quite a sweeping condemnation. This is where assumption meets advice. Of course it may not just be assumption, it may be knowledge hidden in negativity for the opposition. Is the assumption, that farmers are less informed than everyone else? As for being *'just a farmer'* well I believe there are more millionaire farmers than there are millionaire politicians who have become millionaires as a *result* of their politics. As for the advice *'you're better off voting for me'*, based on what? If all a candidate has to offer is bagging the opposition, and this forms part of their spoken platform, the listener needs to recognise this theme of negativity will be deeply embedded in every statement and action they perform.

Assumptions in their conscious form, whether your own or under the influence of others, do not form part of a balanced pit crew, whereas assumptions in their subconscious form do. Remember subconscious assumptions, such as turning up at the supermarket during their opening hours, usually results in being able to do the shopping without a second thought. Well, we don't collect the trolley and think yes, I'm pleased my assumption was correct. We just wander inside and carry on as normal. The subconscious assumption, for the majority of the time, forms part of the pit crew. Conscious assumptions need to be eliminated. Assuming your husband will bring home flowers on your anniversary leads to expectancy. When he turns up with an expensive bottle of red wine instead, your reaction maybe one of excitement and joy, or it may be to question why he's changed the habit of the last ten years. Then the mind can run away with scenarios and assumptions around the absence of the flowers. In a nutshell then, assumptions lead to negative thinking and as we're all about **ELIMINATING NEGATIVITY**, eliminate assumptions. Base decisions on information, data and facts.

The pit crew therefore needs careful selection. You can't change your family but you can make it known some subjects and discussions are off the table and unwelcome. It doesn't matter what people say when they leave the comfort of the restaurant or living room, what matters is the positivity flowing between you all during the meeting, event or gathering. You can choose your friends. Often this leads to calm decisions to move away from those who draw you downwards. Never an easy task, harder as you grow older, but always rewarding. When it comes to the workplace this is harder. We are very often teamed with people we would not choose as friends. The same is true of managers. Given just how much time we spend at work in our lifetime, employment which makes us thoroughly miserable needs to be discarded. We all need to feel valued, and spend our time with like-minded people, or people who support and encourage us. Yes it is easy to fall back to that comforting self-talk, the voices which tell us about how difficult it is to get another job, or where would I get this kind of money, or somewhere else will involve travelling further. However, if a role makes you feel negative, question if it can be flipped, or move on.

The pit crew spreads further. Stop visiting a doctor who makes you uncomfortable or who does not treat you in the way you feel comfortable. The same is true of all such services. If you can't hold a conversation with your hairdresser, find another one. Stop taking less than mediocre servicing from your regular garage. If they can't up their standards to match yours find another mechanic. If you know every time you leave a certain shop the counter crew can't help but offer a '*there she goes*' comment, why are you spending money with them! Pick a pit crew you are proud to recommend and promote.

If your **PIT CREW** is your ultimate support network can you identify the key players?

- List the most positive members of your family, then the most negative.
- When thinking about employment, list the positive influences and the negative.
- In your social or community groups, list the positive influences and the negative.

For the three groups identify the assumptions you have made about the people on either side of the positive / negative spectrum.

- How would you approach the above negative people in future?
- Pre-arm yourself with ways to flip their common arguments.
- Can you replace some of these people with more positive people?

FLY HIGH

YOUR LAST SELF-HELP BOOK

'Through my education, I didn't just develop skills, I didn't just develop the ability to learn, but I developed confidence.'
Michelle Obama

'Inaction breeds doubt and fear. Action breeds confidence and courage. If you want to conquer fear, do not sit home and think about it. Go out and get busy.'
Dale Carnegie

Confidence is like a tree. The roots start to grow early. If the ground is sandy and roots can't gain a good hold, the tree will struggle in the wind and in drought. If the roots grow down into heavy clay they can be constricted and fail to fully mature. A well composted soil allows the roots to spread and mature with time. If the roots fail to effectively mature, the rest of the tree will suffer. It may be green and luscious to look at but inside could be disease or trauma. Branches may be strong or deceptively weak and easy to break and fall. So it is with confidence.

Confidence is derived from the Latin *'to trust'*, so self-confidence could be interpreted as trusting oneself. The aim is to be so confident you can **FLY HIGH** in whatever your do, but not in such a way that you come across as cocky or arrogant.

We gain confidence in a number of ways. At school we might win some athletics events, or do well in the chess club, the mathematics decathlon, be the best at spelling or write the most exciting stories. We may do well at university, for some simply passing the exams lifts confidence yet for others, gaining a high honours award makes them soar. Riding motorbikes might start with a small engine scooter, graduating up the engine sizes to a super sports bike.

FLY HIGH

Managing to ride the scooter promotes confidence to move up to larger bikes. Once the local roads have been mastered, track riding and eventually racing bikes may become the eventual goal. Where skills are required, practice brings proficiency, and proficiency promotes confidence. When we are at the pinnacle of our sport, business, practice or whatever it is we are pursuing we could be said to then be **FLYING HIGH**.

I worked for many years for a US company who developed extraordinary technology infrastructure solutions, mainly in oil and gas, aerospace and mining. As their Problem and Change Management Group Leader, primarily focused on oil and gas, I was part of a team given a project to develop an emergency response centre for a major petroleum company. The project was born out of disaster after a huge gas fire resulted in great loss of life. The sector relies heavily on a multitude of companies and organisations to come together to extract the raw resource, refine it, then on sell. When disaster strikes it usually hits the world's press and never in a positive light. To reduce the likelihood of a similar accident occurring, the major players took the decision an emergency response centre was the most effective way to quickly coordinate emergency services, and mobilise company resources across the sector. Oil and gas is by its nature a highly competitive area. One company does not want to give away any technological advantage or intellectual property so getting a fistful of them to work together for a common safety solution was seen as an incredible, almost impossible challenge. Three years later however, breaking all conventions for competition and business edge, the centre opened its doors.

My company had a culture of positivity. Nothing was impossible and no-one was looked upon in good light if they introduced negativity. What-ifs were almost banned words. It's a challenge when project managing to list contingencies in positive tones, but it's not impossible. A similar approach has to be taken for managing risks. We categorise their likelihood of maturing as high, medium and low, and their effects as high, medium and low. So, a risk might be highly likely to mature but have a low impact. Identifying risks comes with experience, along with many lengthy chats with subject matter experts. Risk of not delivering something on time. Risk of overrunning the budget due to any number of unforeseen circumstances. There is no way on earth to spin all risks in a positive light, but identifying them brings a positive sense of achievement. If the risks are known, the project team know exactly what to look out for. To identify early if the risk is maturing means the previously established contingency plan is ready to mobilise. This is where a negative is flipped to a positive. As with so many career roles, the project manager thrives on success. With every project completed, the lessons learned feed into the individual's self-confidence. Complete enough projects, and the probability of knocking self-confidence reduces. Even small over budget blowouts or time overruns are factored in. The more projects are successfully completed, the more knowledge and wisdom for what will work and what won't add to the levels of self-confidence.

Confidence helps us to establish the building blocks we need for everything else. Having the confidence to flip a negative into a positive. Confidently being able to say no, I don't want to listen to this conversation because you're talking in the negative. Confident enough to build memory modules and to use them. Confident enough to let go of those limiting beliefs. Confident enough to face the roadblock and move past it or to get off the roundabout. Confident enough to make the decision and stick with it, never looking back over it and questioning its validity.

Confidence can also be short-lived and transient. It can be fickle and unpredictable. A task performed a hundred times can out of nowhere, create a sense of foreboding or doom when done for the hundred and first time. When we receive a knock to the confidence, we effectively fall out of the sky. We sink back into self-reflection or introspection and start circling the roundabout again.

Our confidence can be knocked by insults, especially ill-informed insults or verbal attacks. Social media is the perfect breeding ground for insults especially from people who know very little about you, but seem to be quite happy to wade into threads of conversation where often they really have no idea what they're talking about. Don't bother to respond. These types of attacks are not worth the screen they're written on, nor worth the time you've taken to read them. Block or ban the person and ignore. When your confidence is less than perfect, you can be tempted to respond and stab back. It will get you nowhere, and is exactly what the troll needs for food. Most trolls have very little in their lives. They exist in shallow pools of self-reflection thoroughly believing their own rhetoric. Starve them of attention and they will move on. If you challenge them to a verbal duel you will no doubt become ever more infuriated and at some point something will pierce your armour and you'll take a knock to your confidence. So I say again, learn to ignore them. As soon as a troll pops up, block or ban them without so much as a second thought. Remember, **ELIMINATE NEGATIVITY**. Trolls are negative, eliminate them.

I had many a kick to the confidence in my younger years, less so as I've aged. I've already mentioned losing confidence in my left knee and how that affected my ability to ride my motorbike over rough terrain. Solution! Buy a custom fitted knee brace, resulting in the complete return of my riding confidence. Fortunately the older we are the more resilient we become. Every time you meet negativity, flip it to a positive or walk away. If you don't hang around to take the punch, the blow will never connect and dent your confidence.

The workplace is the hardest location to maintain a good level of confidence. It just takes a manager in a bad mood to present a roadblock, or push you onto the roundabout. Either you become stuck behind your declared error and don't know how to move beyond it without managerial guidance, or you're left circling the roundabout trying to figure out where you went wrong. You've been trapped by the negative influence of someone else. Where to now? Flip the negative. Start by writing down precisely what was said. Analyse it and pull it to shreds. Are the comments accurate, a good reflection or misguided? You will arrive at a resolution in your mind. If the comments were justified, grow from it by asking your tormentor what they recommend in order to improve. If the comments were misguided, ask your tormentor what they recommend in order to improve. Yes that's right, the solution is the same no matter what. If you are a subordinate, there is no way to climb above the criticism without challenging the commentator. A challenge will rarely bring respect, but it will attract more negative attention. Acceptance accompanied by a request to improve after pointing out the learning opportunity, is much more likely to attract confidence building praise, than it is to attract further negativity. Now that you've ruminated over it, bounced it around the mind, have you reached resolution? If the answer is yes, set the goal, add it to the roadmap for success, be limitless and go for it. If the answer is no and resolution has not been found well, just how long are you going to spend looking in the rear-view mirror! It's the decision point. Is the criticism large enough it needs a memory module? Will it fit in a toolbox drawer? There comes a point as well you know by now, that ruminating over and over and over a specific topic will bring you nothing but negativity. Put it in a toolbox drawer, give it a curtain call and get off the roundabout.

Someone once said that we only have so many holidays (vacations) available to us. In a way it's true. Those who work full-time for an employer may only have some twenty days of annual leave to use as vacation time. In some countries it is much less. When we are younger we can barely see our way to making age fifty never mind analysing where we want to go on holiday every year. As a university lecturer in the UK leave was almost limitless. With thirty-six days of annual leave which were not tied to out of semester breaks, my whole career there was one long holiday. Well not really, but the compensation by way of leave was incredible. Working in oil and gas was almost a holiday in itself. Every other week was spent in the US or in Europe although there was very little space in the schedules for leisure or family activities.

FLY HIGH

Apart from my multiple holidays to exactly the same island two or three times each year when I was growing up with my grandparents, I truly have no idea where my love of adventure and travel actually came from. Perhaps it was skiing and climbing in different locations and the exposure this gave to different cultures. Perhaps it was growing up with David Attenborough on the television, venturing into jungles and far away deserted islands, sandy cays, deep oceans, rainforests, icescapes and everywhere else my hero has filmed in. Perhaps it was the old master's classic books I sank into with the torch under the bedclothes. *Treasure Island, The Three Musketeers, Jungle Book, Twenty Thousand Leagues, Robinson Crusoe,* or the natural history and wildlife books my grandmother would buy me for Christmas. Or perhaps it's something genetic. My lack of fear gene. My dynamic search for the next great adventure. A trip which goes beyond the normal beach, alcohol and over-eating gluttony.

It is one thing to ride a motorcycle around Scotland, but riding a motorcycle around South America is on the next level. I can't honestly remember how I used to book holidays and adventures. Perhaps it was using old-fashioned technology, the telephone and the pen. Once the internet took flight and the whole world came to the computer screen, never-ending possibilities opened up. I always hunt out my own flights, track down the best deals, sometimes book hotels in advance or more often just the first few nights, book a car, change some currency and go. Where I have had to use a tour company, for South America as an example where border crossings and carnets for motorcycles are often unavailable to individual travellers, research has been my consummate friend. Choosing the most professional and experienced operator for some far away location far outweighs cost.

Over the years I have been rewarded with the confidence to go anywhere, to experience anything, to never doubt my abilities to choose wisely, to hunt out adrenaline experiences and to never think twice before participation. When we decided to scuba dive in Mombasa, I researched a local tour operator in a small village who would take us around Tsavo East and West in the same type of tour bus all of the big companies were using. Same lodges, same game reserves, same tried and tested big game viewing spots and waterholes, but a third of the price, and only four of us in the twelve-seater minibus. The scuba was incredible although less exotic than say the Maldives but every morning our dive boat heading offshore was accompanied by dolphins playing in the bow wave. No decision was a bad decision. Every experience was positive and full on, whether it was bungee jumping in Cairns, leaping off the Auckland tower, standing on the glass floor of the CN Tower in Toronto, taking a helicopter tour of the Grand Canyon, Honolulu, Uluru or an Alaskan glacier, or skiing down the black runs of the Three Valleys in France.

Each experience adds a layer of confidence. Whether it is confidence in booking, selecting, the activity, the adventure, the flight, a train journey, a never before tasted food or meal, unusual drinks, meeting strange animals, or trying to communicate with someone where a language isn't shared. You need confidence in your own ability in order to grow your own confidence in your own ability. No seriously it's true. Be confident in everything you try and everything you do and you will attract more confidence to yourself. Once you taste the pleasure of flying high it becomes a drug you won't want to be without. Yes, life will throw challenges and roadblocks in your direction but with the armour of confidence, you can take the hits because they will bounce off you. The more roadblocks you encounter, the greater the belief in your own abilities you will have, and the easier it will become to shake off the occasional hiccup. Remember, there is no wrong decision, and the rear-view mirror adds nothing to your future.

Practice brings confidence. When you are flying high you are less likely to over analyse, less likely to be self-critical, less likely to get stuck circling the roundabout, and less likely to have to create memory modules. Flying high is a natural partner for positivity. Confidence and negativity do not share the same bed.

- List THREE areas in your past which gave you confidence (sport, awards, achievements, etc.).
- List THREE areas in the present where you feel 100% confident.
- List THREE areas in your present which with a bit of work and practice can be flipped from not so confident to 100% confident.

ACCELERATE YOUR LIFE

YOUR LAST SELF-HELP BOOK

'Our greatest weakness lies in giving up. The most certain way to succeed is always to try just one more time.'
Thomas A. Edison

'If you want to succeed you should strike out on new paths, rather than travel the worn paths of accepted success.'
John D. Rockefeller

'I have learned that success is to be measured not so much by the position that one has reached in life as by the obstacles which he has had to overcome while trying to succeed.'
Booker T. Washington

Remember when your Mum told you to put your jumper on? Not to climb trees? Stay off the road riding your bicycle? Along with a few more dubious comments such as if the wind changes your face will stay like that! In the main, your elders know best. Some of it is generational and experiential common sense. The rest of course might just be a cautious tale so you don't hurt yourself, or more like it, if you climb that tree and fall out and break an arm, I won't be able to live with my own guilt for not being with you every moment of the day. When we're ten, Mum's constant nagging is boring, unnecessary and designed to put a stop to the fun. How we wished we had listened. In amongst the constant Mum-chatter are vital words of wisdom. It seems we have to *live* life in order to accumulate wisdom. Some do develop wisdom earlier than others, yet the majority of people do not expose themselves to enough of life to build their wise armoury.

People do not always naturally gravitate to family and friends when they search for support, which is where a mentor can play a pivotal role. A mentor is not a coach. A coach uses tools and techniques to draw out an individual's goals and guide them along certain paths. A mentor uses their own personal experience as the starting point for guidance. Coaching is technique-based whereas mentoring is more about using lived experience.

Some professional coaches enjoy a celebrity following attracting huge audiences, while commanding significant fees. This kind of mass coaching tends to be a generic one size fits all approach, which is impossible to tailor for individual needs. Topics are broad and not all meet the needs of the attendees. In a vast hall of thousands, all hugging and patting each other on the back, many can be left bemused wondering why they are there.

Mentors come in many forms. Mentoring is not as clear cut as coaching, and certainly not as generic. The ideal is to find a mentor who is a close aspirational fit for the individual seeking assistance. People seeking a mentor must seek a similar profile to their own goals and ideas. There is no point engaging a mentor whose history involves professional sport, when what you need is someone in the aviation industry.

My twenties were lost to idealistic dreams of ski instructing and rock climbing. Coupled with the reality of repetition, other people's poorly behaved children, and far too much après ski activity. I believe that the tedium of my early government role, coupled with the experience of divorce, plus my school mates post-degree high flying careers, made me realise that my grandmother's constant nagging about going to university, was when I should have listened to an elder's perspective. Losing my grandmother so young, meant influential wisdom was lost early, leaving me to float around in the wilderness of *what should I do with my life*? I could have kept going in a dead-end career, but thankfully it is not in my personality to set roots in concrete and not dig them out again. In this life stage I was in a bad marriage and a void absent of influence and guidance. My wisdom came to me through experiential learning.

I can reflect now on where my resilience came from and of course it's obvious. My first twelve years were heavily influenced by two strong and independent grandparents. The next eight years had little parental influence in them at all, living with a very selfish and self-centred mother. My grandmother had me reading all manner of books while I was still in nappies (allegedly). I could read *and* write by the time I started school aged four. I cannot remember if my grandmother who was a school teacher, worked full-time or only part-time. I know my grandfather, as a pit deputy getting closer to retirement was not home much, so I assume he was still working. Was he retired before or after my grandmother died? How the unimportant or impact-less memories fade the fastest. Regardless, my childhood was about reading, playing cards or board games, and when it became cheaper to buy, watching the occasional television program. My grandmother taught me to cook so I always had the confidence to have my hands deep in flour and butter, or throwing something into the oven. Both of my grandparents instilled in me a go-get-it attitude, whereas my mother did not. I can remember answering my mother one year when she asked me what I wanted for Christmas with, 'a bicycle'. 'No, too dangerous,' she replied. Her hair would have turned white had she seen what I got up to at various outdoor activity centres throughout my teens. So, by the time thirteen rolled around and my grandmother had passed away, I already had the resilience necessary to carry me through my teenage years. What I was lacking was guidance. Those fatherly and motherly words which outline possible outcomes of certain actions, which inform the choices we make, reducing the potential for disaster or costly mistakes, were absent. It is this kind of influence which steers us away from misguided marriages, not going to university, poor lifestyle choices, spending too much money when earning so little and pursuing a poor diet, which we need while building up our own book of wisdom.

I made the decision to leave my government job and predictably signed up to a higher diploma then undergraduate degree and on to a master's degree, all successfully completed in the shortest time possible. I say predictably because, with a mantra of **FLYING HIGH**, why would I aim low!

Aiming for high-level qualifications, then moving across career fields rather than sticking to a set career path in a traditional area, refining transferable skills as I have jumped careers, has enriched my working life beyond even my expectations. My skill sets are project management and information systems/ information technology, within a progressive senior management framework. My ultimate aim in my career has not been about climbing a corporate ladder, nor about collecting accolades or rewards through progression and achievement—although I have achieved quite a few—but more about commanding high reward for my skillset. I have worked long hours in some torturous locations including a semi-lawless gas field in Nigeria. Ah Nigeria, where two bottles of Johnny Walker were needed just to bribe my way in and out of Lagos airport. I endured lengthy overseas postings with a single aim, so that I could pursue my life passion, which is travel. Perhaps immersing myself in different cultures around the world is my ultimate way to escape what is stored in my *toolbox*. Couple this with my passion for extreme and adventure sports, my life emphasis has been on the pursuit of income, to support the best upbringing for my son including funding his university fees, and for the pursuit of leisure—not, for everyday living. I often look with wonder at those with shelves filled with shoes or handbags, sheds filled with tools, boats and jet skis parked in the driveway, and five or six bedroomed houses to rattle around in. With wisdom comes the realisation the sum of your life is not in what you own, it is what you have experienced.

Skydiving was my passion for many years. A sport which could never be classified as cheap. Each 'lift', taking a group of skydivers to certain heights (dependant on size of the aircraft and air space restrictions governing maximum jump ceilings) attracts a large fee. Then there is the equipment including the main parachute, the reserve parachute and the harness, container, helmet, gloves, altimeter, full body suit and anything else which is in vogue at the time. Scuba diving has been by far my greatest passion. Training at all levels is extensive and expensive with divers able to specialise in a number of options from sharks, to cold water diving, fish identification, wrecks, drift, deep and many more choices. All of them with different levels of additional equipment and of course additional costs. Then there is the plethora of dive locations. Diving off the same beach once a month would quickly become boring. Most divers seek out new dive locations across the world. This brings high costs. Most practical is to dive off a floating platform, a boat. There are many operators with specialised dive boats (liveaboards) where a week or more is spent entirely at sea moving from dive location to dive location. Not having to return to shore each day allows the boat to explore further away from land often to unspoilt and challenging locations. It is fair to say therefore that adventure and extreme sports are in my blood. Find your passion, be it in your career, your leisure activities, your family or friends or volunteer activities, and you are already in a positive space.

One of my favourite leisure activities is sitting in a café inside a bookstore with a basket full of potential purchases, skimming through the pages while people watching. I love a pile of self-help books. A lot of them are rehashing old theories and techniques. Occasionally something new pops up. I have my favourites, as we all do, but what often disappoints me is the list of tasks and activities they try and convince us to follow in order to help ourselves. Seven techniques, twelve actions, ten habits and so on. In this book you have discovered the one key lesson which drives success in everything else, to **ELIMINATE NEGATIVITY**.

Need some help? Use a mentor. In searching for a mentor, you would not ask an adrenalin junkie to help you define a quieter life so that you can build a business around your passion of knitting and crochet. Your family and your close friends may be wonderful people but are they too close to see the bigger picture? Are there secrets you would prefer to not share with them? Do you have goals which would not be a good fit for their beliefs or culture? Do your desires need refining and defining before revealing them to those closest to you?

Approaching an independent unknown mentor for guidance is the route onto the roadmap for success. Defining your success in isolation can be a laborious process. Engaging a mentor who can show through experience, how to bypass the roadblocks, how to get off the roundabout and most importantly how to **ELIMINATE NEGATIVITY**, could be worth its weight in gold.

I have already mentioned this briefly, and will reiterate it here. If you need a crutch, choose one of the many that already exist. Select from religion, community groups, political parties, social art groups, sports teams, or one of the others. Joining a group will bring you transient or long-term relationships and friendships. From that you may find like-minded people who will share your passion or pastime. Don't however, lose yourself entirely to the cause—allow it to enhance your life, not overtake it. Similarly, if you need a crutch of a professional kind there are many to choose from. There are counsellors, psychologists, psychoanalysts, psychotherapists, mental health coaches of various types, trainers for multiple disciplines, psychiatrists, and many more. Most are trained professionals who deal with specialist fields and specific practice sets. The approach may be to listen to your story and provide a solution tailored only to your needs. Or they may have favourite activities which they mould for all of their clients. The relationship is likely to be formal, professional, and designed to address a specific issue, problem or need.

A mentor, is none of the above, and certainly cannot be classified as a crutch.

Mentoring is about creating a close personal and specific relationship and requires a knowledgeable empathetic and holistic approach looking at everything, including aspirations to build a complete picture. Coaches hop in and out of a person's life or career, a mentor is there to oversee the whole journey.

SUMMARY

I'm guessing you didn't buy this book because you have already reached the pinnacle of success in your life and career! So let's recap on the learning.

- Have you identified your **EVOLUTIONARY MOMENTS?**
- Can you list the moments in your life when you **ACTIVATED CHANGE?**
- Have you identified times where you **ACTIVATED GROWTH?**
- When looking in the **REAR-VIEW MIRROR** did you define your:
    - **ROAD CRASH MOMENTS**
    - **MIDDLE OF THE ROAD MOMENTS**
    - **ULTIMATE ROAD TRIPS**
- What were your **PAST, PRESENT, FUTURE** and **FANCIFUL** patterns and habits that form your **ROUNDABOUTS?**
- Did you identify your **ROADBLOCKS?**
- You can see where you want to go, you just lack the motivation, the impetus or the energy—do you know what **STALLS** you?
- Have you identified your **TANGIBLE GOALS** and your **INTANGIBLE GOALS?**
- We **ELIMINATE NEGATIVITY** by creating **MEMORY MODULES**—have you created at least three?

- Are you able to **VISUALISE** a direction you want to take?
- Are there any specific points in your past where you would need to **REVERSE ENGINEER**?
- Have you fully identified your **PIT CREW**?
- Are you already **FLYING HIGH** or are there gaps?

This book has sought to introduce easy to apply methods for dealing with challenging emotional situations and thoughts, and methods for recognising negative thoughts and flipping them into a positive action. We are all unique. We view and experience life and the world as individuals, but we are influenced by family and friends, employment, education, events, setbacks, barriers, roundabouts, disabilities, disappointments and conditioning. In evolutionary biology terms it is a miracle that we exist at all. We only have one life, and there are no rehearsals. So be the person you really want to be and live a limitless life.

ABOUT THE AUTHOR

Born in the UK, Glynis grew up near Durham, emigrating to Australia in 2007. She now lives off-grid on twenty acres in South Australia with husband Chris, Bob the dog, two alpacas, three sheep, six goats, four chickens, four ducks and 250,000 honey bees.

Glynis is an author, mindset mentor, influencer, adventurer, extreme sport addict, educator, farmer, and freelance learning design consultant. Her professional career spans more than thirty years with senior project management roles in the UK government and in the US oil and gas sector, and as a Principal Lecturer in Information Systems, and Faculty Head of eLearning for Sheffield Hallam University. Since arriving in Australia, Glynis has worked for Charles Sturt University, the NSW Police College, Endeavour Training and Development, Railcorp, ARTC and Pulse Learning.

Glynis has a BSc in Information Technology, a MSc in Decision Support Systems, Graduate Diploma in Writing, Graduate Diploma in Training Management, and Graduate Certificate in Learning and Teaching. Glynis has supervised hundreds of undergraduate and postgraduate students, and professionally mentored countless numbers of her peers.

Glynis rescues wild ducks, runs a busy multi-pronged business, and devotes countless hours each week volunteering in her local community. Glynis never stops learning, and never stops living.

OFFER - 1

CLEAR YOUR HEADSPACE
get started today for FREE

With **FREE** lifetime access to Glynis's MINDSET videos including:

- Start each day in a positive way
- Challenge yourself to recognise your negative thoughts
- Energise your thinking, make every thought count
- Learn techniques for flipping the negative thought into a positive action

Subscribe to Glynis's YouTube Channel
for your monthly inspiration
bit.ly/GlynisTaylorYouTubeChannel

OFFER – 2

FREE YOUR MIND
the Breakthrough Formula for
a Powerful MINDSET

Half-day workshop in a 100% mind-blowing negativity free zone

Includes **FREE** WORKBOOK

- Increase your personal confidence
- Envision a life filled with opportunity
- Revolutionise your state of mind
- Unlock your potential
- Live an extraordinary life

Email *glynis@glynistaylor.com* to learn more about upcoming workshops and dates.

OFFER - 3

BRING POSITIVITY TO YOUR PEOPLE
Presentations and Keynote Speeches

Glynis is a former Problem and Change Management Group Leader and Specialist Project Manager working for some of the world's largest oil and gas sector organisations across Europe, Africa and the United States. She was recruited into academia at the beginning of 2000 and has become a highly skilled and qualified educator, reaching a professional pinnacle in her role as Principal Lecturer in Information Systems, and Faculty Head of eLearning for Sheffield Hallam University in the UK.

Glynis holds a Master of Science in Decision Support Systems. She has travelled to exotic destinations, become totally obsessed with adrenalin and adventure sports, and generally lived an incredible life, but it hasn't always been easy.

Life can throw up some unbelievable challenges and unexpected barriers which can often take a lifetime to overcome. Glynis has committed her personal journey and a lifetime of learning and resulting wisdom to her first book, *Your Last Self-Help Book - A common-sense approach to living life on your terms.*

Glynis has supervised and mentored hundreds of undergraduate and postgraduate students, and professionally mentored countless numbers of her peers.

With her no-nonsense style and calm approach, Glynis is a sought after speaker on the following topics:

1. Unlocking Your Potential
2. Taking Control of Your Thoughts
3. Revolutionise Your State of Mind

Glynis can deliver custom keynotes and presentations between 45 minutes and 3 hours and can be contacted to discuss custom presentations and variations on the above to suit your group or organisation.

Email *glynis@glynistaylor.com* for availabilities and fees.

www.ingramcontent.com/pod-product-compliance
Lightning Source LLC
Chambersburg PA
CBHW021440080526
44588CB00009B/608